CONTENTS

DID YOU KNOW?
For bookworms and
film buffs → p. 23
Fit in the city → p. 48
Favourite eateries → p. 66
Local specialities → p. 70
Time to chill → p. 80
More than a good
night's sleep → p. 98
National holidays → p. 119
Sports – very British → p. 124
Currency converter → p. 125
Weather → p. 126
Budgeting → p. 127

MAPS IN THE GUIDEBOOK
(130 A1) Page numbers and
coordinates refer to the street
atlas
Coordinates are also given for
places that are not marked
on the street atlas
(0) Site/address located off
the map

General map London and
surroundings on p. 146/147

(*A–B 2–3*) refers to the
removable pull-out map

INSIDE FRONT COVER:
The best Highlights

INSIDE BACK COVER:
Public transport map

The best MARCO POLO Insider Tips

Our top 15 Insider Tips

INSIDER TIP Sleepover with dinosaurs

The *Natural History Museum* serves drinks during the late night show and you can even spend the night with dinosaurs → **p. 32**

INSIDER TIP Brunch with drinks

Sign up for the *Bottomless* Sunday brunch in the unique café *Drink, Shop & Do* and guzzle down as much prosecco as you possibly can in two hours → **p. 65**

INSIDER TIP Tea time on the road

B Bakery Bus from Covent Garden takes you on a tour of the city on a genuine Routemaster bus while you indulge in afternoon tea treats → **p. 66**

INSIDER TIP Summer in a car park

Enjoy balmy summer evenings on the roof of a former car park where cool cocktails are mixed in *Frank's Café*. The London skyline is part of the attraction and completely free of charge → **p. 85**

INSIDER TIP Park stop

After a leisurely stroll the pretty park café *Orangery* in Kensington Gardens is just the right place for a nice cup of tea or a glass of Pimm's → **p. 113**

INSIDER TIP Low budget view

Visitors on a tight budget (and everyone else) can experience contemporary art for free and be stunned by the view from the top floor of the *Tate Modern's* new annex → **p. 56**

INSIDER TIP Time travel

Have you ever wondered what a Victorian shopping spree was like? The *Museum of London* presents a typical historical street with shops for you to stroll through → **p. 49**

INSIDER TIP Goodnight!

Charming modern boutique hotel in good location serving organic breakfast for a fair price: that's the *B&B Belgravia* in a nutshell. The studio apartments even have their own kitchens → **p. 94**

INSIDER TIP **Goodbye shopping stress**

Dodge the shopping hordes of Oxford Street! Instead, head for the East End and Shoreditch, which has developed into a shopper's paradise: on *Redchurch Street* and *Cheshire Street* you'll find a mixture of brand name boutiques, indie labels and cranky shops
→ p. 72, 73

INSIDER TIP **High above the Thames**

Nothing for the faint hearted: look down to the Thames far below you through the glass floor on *Tower Bridge's* high walkway. A particular highlight is to see the magic of the bridge lifting beneath your feet
→ p. 109

INSIDER TIP **Authentic India**

It's a long journey to the *Shri Swaminarayan Mandir* (photo left) temple in Neasden but once there you are treated to an impressive temple ceremony and authentic food in the *Shayona Restaurant*
→ p. 60

INSIDER TIP **Flying through the night**

Search the internet for information if you want to go clubbing to contemporary sounds. The hotspots for *Supa Dupa Fly* change on a weekly basis → p. 86

INSIDER TIP **Two masters of music**

Classical and rock under one roof: the events and concerts in the *Handel & Hendrix House* regularly pay homage to both musical geniuses → p. 36

INSIDER TIP **Saturday parliament**

A stroll through the heart of parliamentary democracy: every Saturday, there is a guided tour through the *Houses of Parliament,* the "Mother of all Parliaments" (photo below) → p. 37

INSIDER TIP **Tropical flair**

Amidst tropical greenery the *Skygarden* of the high-rise building *20 Fenchurch Street*, also known as "Walkie-Talkie", offers breathtaking views of the city → p. 51

BEST OF...

FOR FREE

● *The green grass of London ...*
It doesn't have to be a lounge chair for £3.60: many of London's green parks can be used to enjoy a yummy and budget conscious picnic, for example in *Hyde Park* (photo) → p. 30

● *Pedal and save*
The first half hour on the blue bikes of *London's cycle hire network* is free! How about this: cycle to the museum and walk back → p. 122

● *Right royal photo op*
There's no charge for witnessing the changing of the guard in front of *Buckingham Palace* or *Horse Guards Parade*. Lots of bearskin, uniforms, pomp and circumstance for free. The earlier you come, the better the view → p. 35, 36

● *Culture for free*
Watch classic movies, cinematic gems and cult TV series from the national archive at the *British Film Institute*'s mediatheque → p. 87

● *Service in the coronation church*
At £20, the admission charge for Westminster Abbey, the royal coronation church, is fairly steep. If you come during the week for *Evensong* you pay nothing and can still let this magnificent building work its magic on you → p. 38

● *Art and music instead of food*
Instead of lunch: postpone your lunch hour a little and enjoy one of the *free lunchtime concerts* in the church St Martin-in-the-Fields. The art exhibitions in the crypt of the church are free as well → p. 44

● *Temple of the muses, temples of the Gods*
London has a generous museum scene: the *British Musuem*, the fabulous *Victoria & Albert Museum* and *Westminster Cathedral* are all free of charge! → p. 40, 33, 39

◖◗◗◗● Dots in guidebook refer to "Best of ..." tips

ONLY IN LONDON
Unique experiences

● *Because I'm worth it*
The Ritz (photo) is the original and still the best of the classic hotel afternoon teas. Here, in the *Palm Court,* everything is perfect: the atmosphere, the service, the scones → p. 64

● *Bird's eye view*
Only from above does the city reveal itself in its true glory. Look down from the *London Eye,* Europe's tallest observation wheel. A further possibility is the panorama view from *The Shard* → p. 54, 56

● *Dancing*
Dancing through the night: Burn off calories over the weekend on one of the countless dancefloors, e.g. in stylish former bus depot *Ministry of Sound* → p. 86

● *Fish & chips*
Cod, haddock or plaice is battered, fried and served with chips sprinkled with vinegar – a London tradition since the middle of the 19th century. The fish and chips at *Poppies* fish bar are particularly good → p. 67

● *To market!*
Everybody loves London's markets: gourmets head for *Borough Market*, families and East End trendsetters for *Broadway Market* and *Brick Lane Market* – dive right in: browse, look around, buy what takes your fancy → p. 79

● *A pub crawl*
While many pubs have had to close, the city still offers a broad range of drinking dens: Victorian gin palaces, art nouveau ambience, a former posting house or the pub right on the river. Try real ale in the *Black Friar* or *The Dove* → p. 90

● *Double-decker tour*
While London's red double-decker buses have been adapted to a new design, at the core they are still a cheap, authentic means of transport (outside rush hour of course). Whether open-top or covered – the view from the second floor is always excellent and definitely worth a ride → p. 26, 126

ONLY IN

BEST OF...

AND IF IT RAINS?
Activities to brighten your day

● Tea time
At the small but perfectly formed *Postcard Teas* you can sample your way through an authentic tea menu. Go to Saturday tea school at 10am (by appointment) → p. 64

● Curiosity cabinet
Eccentric and wonderfully quirky: the bits-of-everything collection of *Sir John Soane's Museum*. The architect of the Bank of England lived here and gathered together whatever took his fancy. Get in the queue on the first Tuesday of the month to experience the whole thing by candlelight → p. 49

● Bowl 'em over!
Instead of a sweaty beer-soaked ambience, raise a cocktail or a glass of champagne to some US Fifties-style "boutique bowling" at *All Star Lanes*. That's trendy London for you! → p. 84

● Face to face
Take a journey through the centuries with portraits of the most famous people in British history at the *National Portrait Gallery*. Then head to the top floor to stay dry and eat in the *Portrait Restaurant* → p. 43

● London sound
The "listening posts" of *Rough Trade* record store in the East End let you listen to a wide range of musical styles – no hurry, no hassle. And when the rain stops, all Brick Lane is out there waiting for you → p. 80

● Europe's biggest shopping centre
Go on, admit it, shopping is top of your list! With some 350 shops and food outlets, *Westfield* (photo) pulls in the Londoners, and thanks to this mall's clever layout there's not too much of a scrum, allowing for some people-watching as well → p. 72

RAIN

RELAX AND CHILL OUT
Take it easy and spoil yourself

● *Tired of shopping?*
The shopping bags are so heavy that your shoulders are hurting? Why not pop into *Selfridges* (lower ground) for a *walk-in-backrub*? After a refreshing 10-minute massage you'll be ready to go again → **p. 76**

● *Olympic Park fun*
Don't worry, the *Queen Elizabeth Olympic Park* (the reconstructed former Olympic grounds) is not about athletic top performances, it's all strolling, picnics, relaxation and a great view (photo) → **p. 59**

● *Astroshow*
Sink into the lowered seats at the Greenwich Planetarium, best for the live *The Sky Tonight* show: wonderfully calming and relaxing! Just make sure you're not too tired when you go, otherwise ... → **p. 57**

● *Calming the body*
The Oriental Hammam in *Casa Spa* offers steam baths and peelings to cleanse and relax the body; or try English-style treatment at the *Palm Court Chuan Spa* with its tea therapy → **p. 80**

● *Escape into the green*
Out of the city and into nature: take a relaxing trip to peaceful Hampstead and enjoy a stroll through the extensive landscaped park of *Hampstead Heath* → **p. 57**

● *Hotel room with spa*
Stay at the *Fielding Hotel* and kill two birds with one stone: stay centrally in the West End and enjoy free access to the nearby *Covent Garden Fitness and Well Being Centre* → **p. 97**

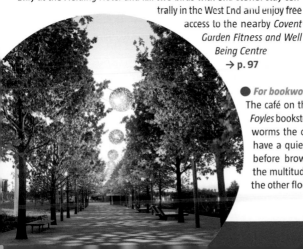

● *For bookworms*
The café on the 5th floor of *Foyles* bookstore gives bookworms the opportunity to have a quiet coffee break before browsing through the multitude of books on the other floors → **p. 74**

INTRODUCTION

DISCOVER LONDON!

People visiting London for the first time harbour certain visual expectations: red double-decker busses, the golden tower of Big Ben, the imposing dome of St Paul's Cathedral, the neo-Gothic towers of Tower Bridge. Those that return for a second or third visit know that the *smorgasbord* known as London includes many additional ingredients, for example crazy fashion trends, and musical subculture, political demonstrations of power in the Houses of Parliament and "the firm" in Buckingham Palace. London is always moving, yet manages to keep its *2,000-year history* alive. It is this contrast between tradition and modernity, between the bearskin hats at the changing of the royal guard and the latest fashion trends on the streets, between afternoon tea at the Ritz and Bengali curries on Brick Lane, that makes the charm of the English, and British, capital. London has 8.6 million inhabitants. This is the centre of British politics, of the financial and media world, of culture — with world-class museums and theatres and a vibrant restaurant scene. International *music and fashion trends* are made here. In the last 20 years London has given itself a fresh coat of paint, with a new skyline, constantly changing quarters, newly styled museums and some of the most ambitious architecture in Europe.

Photo: Millennium Bridge and St Paul's Cathedral

The history of the city began 2,000 years ago as the *Roman trading post of Londinium*. The next occupiers were Anglo-Saxons and Vikings. The victory of the Normans at the battle of Hastings in 1066 to claim succession to the last Anglo-Saxon king, Edward the Confessor, the founder of Westminster Abbey, was the last time that London was conquered. Over the course of the Middle Ages, London grew out of two settlements on the northern bank of the Thames, the City and Westminster, to be a capital of both government and trade. There was never much concern with anything approaching planning. After the flames of the *Great Fire of London* in 1666 had devoured four-fifths of the wooden houses, time and again opportunities for planned urban development were missed, lending the metropolis an engagingly hodge-podge air.

London is a sum of many parts: exclusive Mayfair with fine townhouses, St James's, the quarter of the genteel clubs, the district of Soho with its strip clubs, Bloomsbury, the intellectuals' choice of the 20th century, Spitalfields and Shoreditch, the creative East End, Greenwich with its maritime flair, green Hampstead – a homogeneous whole never emerged. Traditionally Cockneys see themselves as *true Londoners*, born within hearing distance of the church bells of St Mary-le-Bow in the City. Now the idea of a typical Londoner is hard to define. But as early as the 17th century the city was becoming a cosmopolitan city with Huguenot silk weavers arriving from France to avoid persecution. They settled in the East End, and were followed in the 19th century by Irish immigrants looking for work. Then, in the 1950s London received a batch of immigrants from the Caribbean Commonwealth states. They all built up their own social networks, hanging on to parts of their traditions. Others came and went: in 1726, *Voltaire*, the philosopher of French Enlightenment, looked for exile in tolerant London, in the late 19th century *Mahatma Gandhi* was inspired by British socialists and the dramatist *George Bernard Shaw* during his legal studies here, and Hampstead was to be the last residence of *Sigmund Freud*, fleeing Nazi persecution. Today, just look around you in the tube for a cross-section of London's population: a City manager in pinstripes next to a dreadlocked Afro-Caribbean teenager, an old

A cosmopolitan mosaic

Catch your own bouquet at the Columbia Road flower market

Chinese lady, a young skater in sports designer labels next to a Bengali mother in a sari. The bomb attacks in 2005 have done little to dent the openness and multi-cultural lifestyle of the city.

"London" does not equal "England", but some English character traits – a certain reserve, politeness, a tolerant individualism, a sense of tradition, understatement, paired with self-deprecation – form the foundation for coexistence in the metropolis. No less than *thirty cultures* share this city; over a third of Londoners belong to an ethnic minority. Only 40 minutes from Trafalgar Square, in the suburb of Southall, you can imagine yourself in the Punjab, between Indian radio music, shops selling *salwar kameez* and curry aromas. *300 languages* are spoken in the capital of the mother country of the English language, a reminder of the *British Empire* which, during the reign of Queen Victoria (1837–1901), stretched across a quarter of the globe. But it's not all smiles: tabloid newspapers bring up the topic of immigration time and again, especially since the referendum in June 2016, in which the UK voted to leave the EU. London, however, voted against Brexit – hardly surprising in a city in which only 45 per cent of the population classify themselves as "white and British".

> **Multicultural yet very British ...**

Londoners earn £750 per week on average but incomes vary greatly depending on which part of town you live in. With Kensington & Chelsea and Tower Hamlets, London can claim both the richest and the poorest areas in the country. The unemployment rate is declining and currently just under 6 per cent. While Londoners are not yet much into recycling, more and more cycle to work and *volunteer*: maybe reforesting at a *Green Gym* in the park or as a mentor working against the gang ideology of carrying knives but not schoolbooks. *Doing something for the community* is becoming ever more important as central services fall victim to budget cuts. Londoners are politically and culturally interested and use iPods and e-readers to shorten their commute to work.

Day-to-day life in the metropolis

London's old nickname, *the Big Smoke*, is a reminder of the time when industrial smog was still claiming lives. In fact, London boasts more *green spaces* than any city of comparable size. Pleasant walks lead through Hyde Park, Green Park or Regent's Park, where office workers unwrap their sandwiches in their lunch break. The *royal parks* are only one example of the historical legacy of the monarchy; the royals may bring lots of tourists into the city, but for day-to-day life the Queen has a lot less significance than the manager of Arsenal football club or the latest development in the soap opera *Eastenders*. In 2011 middle-class Kate Middleton was accepted into the inner circle of the royal family. However, in 2012 the focus of the media and the population at large was the Queen, who celebrated her *Diamond Jubilee* with many events. A year later, the royal baby Prince George was born, and in 2015, Princess Charlotte, the youngest member of the royal family.

For their immediate day-to-day needs Londoners count on their mayor, Sadiq Khan. His most difficult tasks are getting citizens from A to B and creating new affordable housing. Every year, the *world's oldest and longest underground network* transports a billion passengers, fighting technical problems. The tube stations of the *Jubilee Line* might resemble cathedrals, but traffic in the city with Europe's most expensive public transport system is still often near breaking point – despite the congestion charge. The "Cross Rail Project" will hopefully alleviate the problem. This east-west route, running underground from Heathrow airport to the financial district of Canary Wharf is expected to be in operation by the end of 2019. The second most discussed subject is the housing situation. London's *real estate prices* are the highest of all European cities. In noble quarters like Chelsea, a two-bedroom flat will cost around £800,000. Houses can easily cost tens of millions and many properties are bought by foreign investors. So most Londoners have no chance of finding affordable, reasonably central accommodation. The hunt for cheap living space was also behind the Hoxton, Shoreditch, Dalston and Hackney phenomenon of recent years, when artists and others leading more alternative lifestyles moved into these crumbling parts of town near the City, turning them into trendy places. "Trendy" here is not meant in the way of gentrified Notting Hill. Walking between kebab takeaways, pound shops, walls pasted over with fly-posters and plastic bags blown about by the wind brings on more of a high noon feeling. These unvarnished areas of east London, full of young people, cultivate their own kind of snobbery. In a fast-moving scene, they know which grubby façade hides steps down into the latest club. Areas south of the Thames, like Clapham and Peckham, are also on the rise.

The best place to feel the pulse of London is along the *Thames*. Londoners have re-discovered the river for strolling. The murky waters deceive: *Father Thames* is cleaner than it has been in the past 50 years, and bridges — modernised (Hungerford Bridge) and new (Millennium Bridge) — give the city a new sense of cohesion. The river has always marked the dividing line between the financial and the governmental districts on the north bank and south London. *Sarf'* London, to date known for anonymous social housing and a lack of infrastructure, has gained ground and is inspiring *new trends* and urban sounds. The model quarter here is Southwark, since 2012 endowed with Europe's second-tallest building, Renzo Piano's office tower *The Shard*. There are further skyscrapers under construction in Vauxhall and Battersea. The east of the city has also been rejuvenated as a result of the 2012 Olympic Games: the Olympic grounds have been converted into Queen Elizabeth Olympic Park. It is this dynamism that makes London one of the world's most fascinating cities.

Where true trends are born

Commuter ready to jump aboard the underground

WHAT'S HOT

1 London in bloom

Green city ✿ Too little space for nature? Organisations such as London's *Guerilla Gardening* group are not that bothered. At night they turn their city green with sunflower and other seeds *(www.guerrillagardening.org) (photo)*. For sporty vibes check *Trees for Cities*: events such as the Run for Trees raise money to finance the planting of new trees and protection for old ones *(www.trees forcities.org)*.

Home-made!

2

Beer, cheese, pasta, sausages Many Londoners love home-made products and try to stay away from boring homogenous supermarket food. "Keep local" is the motto. Farmers heed the call and sell organic produce such as pasta, pies, bread, fruit juices and sausages at weekly markets *(www.lfm. org.uk)*. William Oglethorpe doesn't own a dairy farm but produces organic cheese in London all the same *(www.kappacasein.com)*. For the thirsty there's plenty of craft beer which has become all the rage in London pubs. It is brewed locally in small quantities and comes in all kinds of flavours from fruity to bitter *(craftbeer london.com)*.

3 Dining differently

Living-room atmosphere Supper clubs such as *Leluu's Supper Club (www.leluu.com)* are booming. On their website you can receive an invitation on request and then get served at Leluu's home. The latest trend to hit London is hideaway bars behind camouflaged doors and secret rooms in cocktail clubs which you enter through a mirror or even a fridge *(www. designmynight.com/london/bars/secret-bars-in-london)*. For more clubs check out *www.londonpopups.com*.

There are lots of new things to discover in London. A few of the most interesting are listed below

Feel-at-home café

Money is time   London's coffee shop chains now have competition from living room-style cafés where guests are invited to feel at home. Everything is free inside the Shoreditch coffee shop *Ziferblat (388 Old St. | london.ziferblat.net)* including the coffee (which you make yourself), biscuits and WiFi: you only pay for the time you spend there. This is a place to feel at home and meet up with friends. For £3 an hour (5 pence a minute) you can drink as much coffee as you like while surfing the net. The feel-good factor is also felt in the *Nana Café (The Convenience| Brooksby's Walk | www. wearenana.com):* traditional food reminiscent of your childhood is served up in Hackney by a caring team of old yet young-at-heart ladies. Or how about a slice of legal advice served with your coffee at *The Legal Café (81 Haverstock Hill | Hampstead | www.81haverstockhill. com)?* At *Lock 7 (129, E2 Pritchard's Road | Hackney | lock-7.com)* have your bicycle repaired while you relax over a cup of coffee.

4

Night owls

5

Splash!   How about some nocturnal aquatic adventures by canoe or kayak on the Thames (photo) or with swimming goggles in a lido? This are the perfect activities for night owls and people who love surprises and want to take their social life offline and outside for a change. Swim together by the light of the moon and huddle around a campfire for warmth afterwards. Or kayak under Tower Bridge and then climb the fire escape to regain strength at the pub. For Halloween there's a scary boat trip on Regent's Canal. All this and more is organised by *Secret Adventures (tel. 32 87 79 86 | secretadventures.org)*.

IN A NUTSHELL

THE ROYAL FAMILY ...

is still a favourite topic of the tabloids but there just isn't as much to gossip about as in the 1990s when Queen Elizabeth II and Prince Philip's offspring produced scandals by the minute: divorce, adultery, petty quarrelling – you name it. Even "Dirty Harry", second son of Charles and Diana, who used to love dropping a clanger, has calmed down and nowadays promotes charities for war veterans, lately making the headlines when he married the actress Meghan Markle in May 2018. His older brother, Prince William, who married long-time girlfriend, commoner Kate Middleton, several years ago, has already produced the expected heirs with the birth of three children so far.

But what makes the British royals so fascinating to visitors from other countries? Is it the glitz and glamour of kings and queens, princes and princesses in general? The marches and ceremonies that are perfectly staged with costumes, bearskin hats and much ado? Or a bit of nostalgic yearning in our romantic little hearts for the story of Cinderella and Prince Charming? One major attraction of the British monarchy is surely Queen Elizabeth II herself. Her staying power commands respect – she has

Multicultural mix, monarchy, music & more – new trends rock the city without cutting off ties with the past

been ruling with pertinacity and discipline for over 65 years now. Even at over 90 she still appears at many public functions and events. Such a sense of duty and commitment in someone her age is truly admirable.

MULTICULTURAL
Next to New York, London is THE multicultural capital of the world. As a new visible sign of their diversity, Londoners voted for Sadiq Khan to become their new Lord Mayor in May 2016 – a novelty in the history of the city as lawyer Khan is the child of Pakistani immigrants and the first ever Muslim major of London. The son of a bus driver, he grew up in the ethnically diverse district of Tooting in the south of London and his insight into the woes and sorrows

tural London a place worth living in for people of all kinds of backgrounds.

R OYAL JELLY

The extensive grounds behind Buckingham Palace abound in flower beds and shrubs, winding paths and hedgerows, a tennis court, a small lake, garden pavilions and old trees.

Two sycamores standing side by side have grown so large that their branches are now intertwined – a beautiful symbol for a happy couple as these trees were planted by Victoria and Albert, the great-great-grandparents of the Queen. The garden side of the palace looks out on a lawn with fresh green grass which becomes the location for very special events in summer: royal garden parties.

A selection of people who have attained special achievements for their country, i. e. in the realm of sport, voluntary work or other areas, are invited to one of the Queen's annual three big garden parties. On these occasions about 8,000 guests trample the well-groomed lawn, scoffing 20,000 pieces of cake and as many sandwiches, all washed down with 27,000 cups of tea. There are plenty of insects buzzing about but luckily no one needs to fear mosquito bites as most of them are bees from New Zealand which the Queen keeps on the small island in the lake.

A toast to the Commonwealth: these insects not only produce up to 400 jars of royal honey per year but are also less aggressive than their British cousins. After all, it wouldn't do at all if the Queen's guests were suddenly attacked by a swarm of royal bees ...

P OOR DJS

The Swinging Sixties are long gone but London is still a hotspot of good music. Popular musical genres like garage, hip-hop, drum & bass or r'n'b are con-

Adele – top pop export from Tottenham

of less privileged people is based on his personal experiences – which makes him just about the opposite of his predecessor, the often foppish Boris Johnson. Johnson went to Eton and Oxford, comes from a white, elitist background and was well connected in the Conservative Party. Sadiq Khan, a member of the Labour Party, is now facing many challenges and must undertake numerous adjustments in order to make multicul-

stantly evolving; rock turns into heavy electro rock and electronic music is mixed with elements of jazz and blues. This is the place where trends are made and musicians are born that in days to come will form a school band and play live in clubs after they have had a few hits on YouTube. Camden has now been at the heart of the music scene for over 50 years. Musical greats like The Rolling Stones and Jimi Hendrix gave memorable performances in the legendary *Roundhouse*. Blur, Oasis, Suede, Amy Winehouse, David Bowie and Pink Floyd all used to play in Camden. Adele from Tottenham in North London is one of the stars of the younger generation. She was awarded an Oscar, a Grammy and a Golden Globe for the title song of James Bond movie *Skyfall*. In the autumn of 2015 she conquered the global charts with her heartfelt love song "Hello". In fact, the song was so successful that it was played on the radio for weeks on end – very much to the annoyance of the long-suffering DJs.

IT'S TEATIME

Don't worry: You don't *have* to drink tea on your visit to London. Apart from the big coffee chains, there are lots of small, often unusual *coffee houses*. Still: for Brits in general and Londoners in particular tea is the (non-alcoholic) consoling drink of choice in crises of all sorts. After a nice hot "cuppa" your problems just seem that tiny bit more bearably. On a daily basis British tea drinkers opt for the express version: teabag, hot water, a spot of milk, done! Luckily, this is not the case when you order afternoon tea in a hotel or café where the fine

FOR BOOKWORMS AND FILM BUFFS

Rush of Blood – Mark Billingham's crime novel (2014) of a psychodrama which develops between three London couples during a series of dinner parties

London NW – tragicomedy (2014) by Zadie Smith. An in-depth portrayal of the everyday reality of multicultural inhabitants in this London district

Paddington – British film comedy (2014) which tells the heart-warming story of everyone's favourite bear from Peru. Paddington comes to London and finds a new home with the Brown family (Hugh Bonneville, Sally Hawkins) but wreaks quite a bit of havoc on the way. Fond portrayal of London with

spectacular show down at the Natural History Museum

Sherlock – The BBC TV series (since 2011) delivers a modern-day interpretation of the unlikely crime-solving duo of Holmes (played by Benedict Cumberbatch) and Watson (played by Martin Freeman)

Bridget Jones' Baby – Romantic comedy (2016) with heaps of London charm and the blundering but lovable protagonist Bridget (Renée Zellweger). This time around Bridget's chaotic love life oscillates between two men – Mark Darcy (Colin Firth) and Jack Qwant (Patrick Dempsey) – while we wonder who the father of her baby is

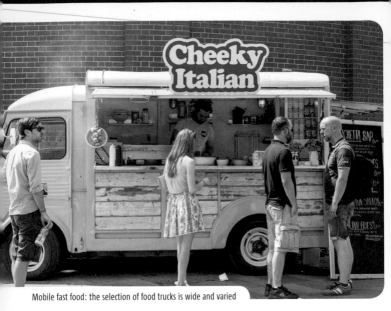

Mobile fast food: the selection of food trucks is wide and varied

art of tea drinking is held high and loose tea leaves are used for the freshly brewed tea which is served with a pot of hot water for a second infusion, milk of course and a nice array of delicious sandwiches and cakes.

POP UP!

It may sound like an instruction for reluctant corn kernels in a hot pan, but in London (and other large cities) the word "pop-up" rings other bells: just like corn, a new store will pop up somewhere in town unannounced and sell trendy clothes for a few weeks. Or a bar will emerge on a rooftop for a limited period of time and spread seasonal love with winter scenery or a summer garden, serving food and drinks while providing protection from the potentially inclement weather. A young designer may use an old shipping container as a temporary abode from which to promote his new business plan. And per-

haps a whole container village will be celebrating outlandish culinary creations and original cocktails in the summer while growing an experimental garden and selling crazy shirts. You should definitely pop up and check it out! *www. londonpopups.com | www.popbrixton. org | www.boxpark.co.uk*

MEALS ON WHEELS

We know "meals on wheels" as a service delivering more or less tasty food to old people who can no longer cook for themselves. The meal delivery service for young Londoners is quite a different kettle of fish. And it's not actually delivered, you have to go get it yourself: street food!

Trucks and vans in all shapes and sizes put fresh, healthy, savoury, sweet and above all unusual food on your plate or into your take-away box. You can try everything on the go, from Thai to African, from Italian to Spanish, and from Korean to German. So why not go on a culinary journey around the world and taste your way through London's food trucks and street food stands? You will find them in the streets and markets of Clapham, Camden, Notting Hill or Bethnal Green. Bon appetit! *londonstreetfoodie.co.uk*

B RUNCH WITH EXTRAS

Boring old-fashioned breakfast was yesterday – say hello to brunch! This mixture between breakfast and lunch has become the preferred weekend meal for many Londoners.

Now there's a new variety that's immensely popular: the *bottomless brunch*. Sounds a bit raunchy but the "bottom" actually refers to the bottom of a glass rather than a person's derrière. The idea was to transport the happy hour from early evening to mid-morning: You pay a fixed price for Prosecco and cocktails and then have a time slot of one or two hours in which to down as many glasses as possible. Oh, and you can also order some food ... Those who love to sing can then move on to a hip-hop brunch – it's much easier to stand up in front of an audience and sing karaoke with a bit of alcohol running through your blood. *www.hiphopbrunchldn.com*

K EEP YOUR EYE ON THE CATHEDRAL

Visitors to London sometimes notice that the city's tower blocks are arranged in a strange way – as if following a secret pattern you can't quite make out. The pattern only becomes obvious when climbing one of the hills surrounding London like *Primrose Hill* or *Hampstead Heath*. From there you get a great view of the city with *St Paul's* and *Westminster Cathedral*. And that explains the

mystery: the view to these historic landmarks, especially to the cathedral, must not be blocked which effectively means that no new high-rise buildings can be erected along certain corridors and visual axes. Thus the cathedral is also visible from *Henry's Mound* in Richmond. Even though it is 16 km away, it can be seen through a gap in the shrubbery with the naked eye on a clear day or through a telescope when the sky is overcast.

M ORE THAN JUST A GAME

22 players divided into two teams run after a ball and try to kick it into the opponent's goal. Of course, no one would describe football (called "soccer" in the USA, Australia and New Zealand) in such simplistic terms in the motherland of the game. The first ball games of this kind were probably already played in England in the Middle Ages.

What can be historically verified is the founding of the first official football club in the year 1857 (Sheffield Football Club); shortly afterwards the Football Association (FA) was founded. The three big clubs in London – Arsenal, Chelsea and Tottenham – are not only masters of the game on the field but also experts in buying and selling star players from and to other international clubs – for bucket loads of money, needless to say (tickets see box p. 124). And managers are shed almost as quickly as sweaty shirts after a game – except for one: Arsenal have stuck with the same manager – Arsène Wenger – for over 20 years now. The Frenchman is not only considered to be a great manager but also a clever scout for new talent; plus he doesn't spend the club's money recklessly and even participated in the design of the new Emirates Stadium. Arsenal fans love and express this in their motto "Arsène knows!"

SIGHTSEEING

WHERE TO START?

CITY **WHERE TO START?**
Trafalgar Square (142 A1)
(⌖ J–K6): The relevant tube and train station is Charing Cross (Northern/Bakerloo Line), 100 m away, and many buses pass here. Walking down Whitehall takes you to the Houses of Parliament and Big Ben, the London Eye and the attractions on the bank of the Thames in 10 minutes. A brisk walk through St James's Park brings you to Buckingham Palace in no time, art fans have the National Gallery right there; music lovers go to St Martin-in-the-Fields.

It's true: London's visual and sensual overload can be too much for the visitor. Don't try and see everything at once; hopefully, this won't be your last time in town!

Countless city monuments can be seen for free; where there is a charge to pay, it is often quite steep, however.

Visitors can still experience the original red ● double-decker buses on two *Routemaster Heritage Routes (9 and 15)*. Bus routes 11, 23, 24, 38, 205 and 390 pass some more city highlights.

If you're lucky you can find an empty seat on the top deck of one of the Routemaster buses that have been newly designed by Heatherwick.

Fabulous architecture, stone witnesses to a chequered history, palaces, green oases and famous museums

Thames boats offer pretty panoramic views and connect many attractions. A trip with the fully automatic *Docklands Light Railway (DLR)* is an excellent way to see the new London that has grown up in the east *(www.dlr.co.uk)*. Excellent city tours are on offer e.g. from *Original London Walks (tel. 76 24 39 78 | www. walks.com)*. INSIDER TIP Unusual tours, including Harry Potter film location tours or a Beatles Walk, cost about £10 per person.

London boasts some of the most important permanent art collections in the world. A long history and the expansion of the British Empire, as well as the Victorians' enthusiasm for collecting, have endowed the city with a unique museum landscape.

Londoners themselves like to visit museums, maybe because even the most prestigious institutions don't just ride the high horse of serious education, they offer many interactive experiences

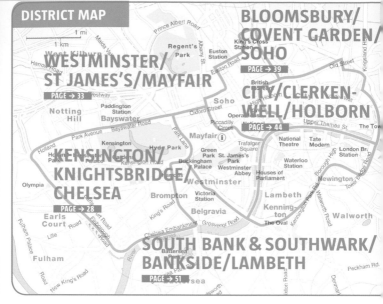

DISTRICT MAP

BLOOMSBURY/
COVENT GARDEN/
SOHO
PAGE → 39

WESTMINSTER/
ST JAMES'S/MAYFAIR
PAGE → 33

CITY/CLERKEN-
WELL/HOLBORN
PAGE → 44

KENSINGTON/
KNIGHTSBRIDGE/
CHELSEA
PAGE → 28

SOUTH BANK & SOUTHWARK/
BANKSIDE/LAMBETH
PAGE → 51

The map shows the location of the most interesting districts. There is a detailed map of each district on which each of the sights described is numbered.

too. Most museums have free admission; what can make a visit expensive are special exhibitions, the museum cafés and those enticingly presented *gift shops*.

The Tate Modern offers extended opening times at the weekend, other museums at specific days of the week. The *www.culture24.org.uk* webpage carries up-to-date information on opening times and current special exhibitions. During the opening times of Tate Britain and Tate Modern, the **INSIDERTIP** ▶ *Tate Boat (one way with Travelcard £5 | tel. 78 87 88 88)*, a catamaran with Damien Hirst's colourful polka dot design, shuttles every 40 minutes between these two top museums.

KENSINGTON/ KNIGHTS- BRIDGE/ CHELSEA

A lot of green spaces, top-class shops and temples of culture dominate this quarter. Chelsea, on the northern bank of the Thames, only has a few scattered tourist attractions, but it was the centre of "Swinging London" in the 1960s and punk in the 1970s.

Chelsea has remained one of the top residential addresses in town, today however more high society than bohemian society. Football fans know Chelsea as the home of one of the richest clubs in the Premier League.

Club owner Roman Abramovich and other beautiful and/or wealthy inhabitants don't have far to go to the shopping mile of King's Road or the consumer palaces of Harrods and Harvey Nichols in Knightsbridge. In the 1980s, the area around Sloane Square was dominated by Diana Spencer and other young wealthy *Sloanies*. In 2008 the move of the Saatchi Gallery brought a breath of fresh air. South Kensington boasts several magnificent museums within a small area, flanked by small shops, restaurants, patisseries and London's French school. The extensive green spaces of Hyde Park and Kensington Gardens attract walkers, skaters and deckchair loungers.

1 ALBERT MEMORIAL
(139 E2) (*ω D7–8*)

Queen Victoria's beloved husband Albert of Saxe-Coburg-Gotha died in 1861 at the age of 42. The neo-Gothic monument (1876), adorned with marble, mosaic glass and semi-precious stones, was created by George Gilbert Scott whose grandson Giles designed the red phone box. The statue shows Albert with the catalogue of the *Great Exhibition* of 1851, at his feet a frieze with figures from the arts and sciences. *Guided tours (45 min.) March–Dec 1st Sun in month 2, 3pm | £8 | Kensington Gardens | www.royalparks. org.uk | tube Central: Lancaster Gate*

◻2 CHELSEA PHYSIC GARDEN
(0) (*
 F11*)

London's most hidden garden, established in 1673 for students of medicine. Stroll amongst the beds with pharmaceutical

◻4 HYDE PARK ●
(140 A–C 1–2) (*
 E–F 6–7*)

London's largest and most famous park. On *Rotten Row* you might see high society on horseback while at *Speakers' Corner*

Hyde Park: one of London's green spaces

plants from all over the world, the rock garden and historic teaching garden. In Aug/Sept there is honey for sale. *April– Oct Tue–Fri 11am–6pm, Sun 11am–6pm | £9.90 | free guided tours | Swan Walk | 66 Royal Hospital Road | www.chelsea physicgarden.co.uk | tube Circle, District: Sloane Square*

◻3 CHEYNE WALK (0) (*
 D–E11*)

Stroll along historic residences on the Thames from the 17th and 18th centuries. Amongst the illustrious past residents are Sir Thomas More, Henry VIII's Lord Chancellor, the painter and poet Dante Gabriel Rossetti, footballer George Best and singer Mick Jagger. *www.rbkc.gov.uk | tube Circle, District: Sloane Square*

(132 B6) (*
 F6*) *(tube Central: Marble Arch)* anybody and everybody has been allowed to say what they like since 1872. This is also the only place in Great Britain where political demonstrations may congregate without police authorisation; it is the starting point for all marches. Next to the *Serpentine Bridge*, the *Diana, Princess of Wales Memorial Fountain* (139 F2) (*
 E7*) is an elegant construction, a granite ring with water features. *Tube Piccadilly: Hyde Park Corner, Central: Marble Arch, Lancaster Gate, Queensway*

◻5 KENSINGTON PALACE
(139 D2) (*
 C7*)

Princess Diana's residence after her separation from Prince Charles, now

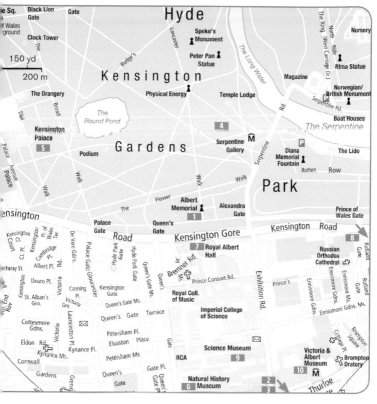

SIGHTSEEING IN KENSINGTON/KNIGHTSBRIDGE/CHELSEA

1 Albert Memorial
2 Chelsea Physic Garden
3 Cheyne Walk
4 Hyde Park

5 Kensington Palace
6 Natural History Museum
7 Royal Albert Hall
8 Saatchi Gallery

9 Science Museum
10 Victoria & Albert Museum

Princes Harry and William and the latter's wife, Catherine, live here. There is now an exhibition on Queen Victoria. The State Apartments display clothing owned by Lady Di. INSIDERTIP Entrance to the inner palace café area is free. *March–Oct daily 10am–6pm, Nov–Feb up to 4pm | £16.50 | www.hrp.org.uk | tube Circle, District: High Street Kensington*

6 NATURAL HISTORY MUSEUM
(139 E–F4) (*D9*)

With its light-blue and pinkish terracotta bands and thousands of ornamental sculptures of animals and plants, the monumental Natural History Museum is arguably the prettiest museum building in town. A 85-foot-long Diplodocus dinosaur skeleton forms the centrepiece of the cathedral-like Hintze Hall. The idea is that natural history doesn't have to be boring. Thanks to high-tech sensors the life-like dino model of a Tyrannosaurus Rex follows your movements! The *Earth Galleries* simulate the 1995 earthquake that shook Kobe in Japan in a reconstructed supermarket. The Images of Nature gallery shows stunning photographs and paintings; the interactive film on evolution is no less stunning.

In a spectacular annexe, the *Darwin Centre* displays zoological rarities, malformations and curiosities in glass jars. The *Spirit Collection Tour (£10 | children from 8 years upwards)* presents giant squid "Archie" – a whopping 8.50 m/28 ft long! *Party animal lates* serves drinks and food every last friday of the month *(6pm– 10pm)*. Free admission, but tickets *(from £15)* required for some events. Feel like spending the night with a dino? Then check out the available sleepover dates of INSIDER TIP ▶ *Dino Snores* for families with

kids aged 7 to 11. *Daily 10am–5:50pm | free admission | Cromwell Road | www. nhm.ac.uk | tube Circle, District, Piccadilly: South Kensington*

🔳7 ROYAL ALBERT HALL
(139 E3) (*𝄞 D8*)

Inaugurated in 1871, the famous brick-red circular concert hall today puts on a broad programme. *Theme based tours on different days, also available with champagne or afternoon tea (online reservation strongly recommended) | £12.75 | tel. (0)84 54 01 50 45 | www.royalalberthall. com | Kensington Gore | tube Circle, District, Piccadilly: South Kensington*

🔳8 SAATCHI GALLERY
(140 B5) (*𝄞 F9–10*)

Advertising mogul Charles Saatchi, for a long time one of the most important promoters of new British artists, today shows more international contemporary art: paintings and installations. *Daily 10am–*

You just can't miss it: the dinosaur skeleton in the Natural History Museum

6pm | free admission | Duke of York's Head-quarters, King's Road/Sloane Square | www.saatchi-gallery.co.uk | tube Circle, District: Sloane Square

▣9 SCIENCE MUSEUM (139 F4) *(ሕ D8)*
This museum dedicated to the sciences brings the rapid development of technical achievements to life: from the first steam locomotive, "Puffing Billy" (1813), the *Burnley Mill Engine*, whose huge wheel once powered 1,700 weaving looms, to a reconstruction of the Apollo moon landing capsule. For a more hands-on approach step into the flight simulator *(£6)*. A 3D-movie lets you fly to the moon with the Apollo or dive into the ocean *(£5–6 each)*. Who am I? What will I look like when I grow old? What would my voice sound like if I changed gender? Discovering and experimenting is encouraged in the gallery "Who am I". Nerds can play the first ever home video game "Pong" in the gallery "The Secret Life of the Home". And those that love the ticking of old clocks can admire the 400-year-old art of timekeeping and over 1,000 chronometers in the *Clockmakers' Museum. Daily 10am–7pm | free admission | Exhibition Road | www.sciencemuseum.org.uk | tube Circle, District, Piccadilly: South Kensington*

▣10 VICTORIA & ALBERT MUSEUM ●
(139 F4) *(ሕ D–E 8–9)*
This museum, V&A for short, is the world's largest for the decorative arts: sculptures, china, fashion, furniture, glass, silver, sacred art from Europe, America and Asia. Look into the *British Galleries* and not only see complete interiors, but also pieces of the Arts and Crafts Movement and art nouveau of William Morris and Charles Rennie Mackintosh, but also King James II's wedding suit (1673). The 24 m/78 ft high *Cast Courts*

showcase large sculptures (among them a replica of Michelangelo's David). There are other exhibitions to see along with the museum's collection. Stunning: the V&A Café with its intricately decorated glass windows and pillars. *Daily 10am–5:45pm, Fri parts of the collection up to 10pm | daily free guided tours at 10.30am, 12.30pm, 1.30pm, 3.30pm | admission free | Cromwell Road/Exhibition Road | www.vam.ac.uk | tube Circle, District, Piccadilly: South Kensington*

WEST-MINSTER/ ST JAMES'S/ MAYFAIR

Meet the London of the postcards, the conservative "Establishment" and, let's face it, the stereotypes.
Westminster, as the western core of old Londinium from which London grew and the counterpart to the City, concentrates the temples of secular and spiritual power: parliament, palaces and splendid cathedrals.
Doors closed to mere mortals hide the world of the genteel gentlemen's clubs of St James's, a London pied-a-terre for the nobility and a networking place for Old Boys, who know each other from attending the right schools and universities. Think leather armchairs in wood-panelled rooms. However, since 2007, the smoke rising up from the decision-makers' pipes has been a thing of the past: private clubs are not exempt from the smoking ban! In the green oases of St James's Park and Green Park you too can beat the stress of the city – get a deckchair and take a deep breath! Mayfair is the

most expensive property on London's Monopoly board; small wonder then that Madonna bought not one but several houses here. Wealthy young students, managers and princes now rent the villas which were mainly offices in the past and have turned the district into a party zone. But embassies, chic hotels, nightclubs and classy shopping streets that want nothing to do with the shopping drag of nearby Oxford Street, also prevail.

■ BANQUETING HOUSE
(142 A2) (*∅ K7*)

The huge Whitehall Palace burned down in 1698, and all that remains of it is this neoclassical building by Inigo Jones. In front if it, Charles I of the Stuart dynasty was beheaded in 1649. Charles had commissioned Peter Paul Rubens with the magnificent ceiling paintings on the first floor: they glorify the reign of his father, James I, using rich symbolism. *Daily 10am–5pm | £6, children under 16 free |* *Whitehall | www.hrp.org.uk | tube Jubilee, Circle, District: Westminster*

■ BUCKINGHAM PALACE ★
(141 D–E3) (*∅ H8*)

When Elizabeth II is at home, the red-gold-blue Royal Standard flag flies from the roof of this massive neoclassical building; if not, then the Union Jack takes its place. In August and September, while the Queen is summering in Scotland, two dozen of the over 700 rooms are open to the public (*£21.50 incl. audioguide, duration 2–2.5 hours | www.royalcollection.org.uk*). A permanently accessible part of the palace is the *Queen's Gallery (daily 10am–5:30pm | £10.30)* with the treasures of the huge royal collection of Old Masters, and the royal stables, *Royal Mews* (141 D3) (*∅ H8*) (*Feb–March, Nov Mon–Sat 10am–4pm, April–Oct daily 10am–5pm | £9.30 (incl. audioguide)*), with Her Majesty's horses. Vintage car fans will have a ball as the INSIDER TIP royal car fleet is

Magnificent coats-of-arms adorn the gates of Buckingham Palace

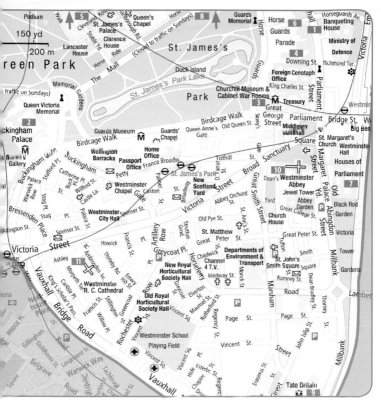

SIGHTSEEING IN WESTMINSTER/ST JAMES'S/MAYFAIR

1. Banqueting House
2. Buckingham Palace
3. Churchill War Rooms
4. Downing Street
5. Handel & Hendrix House
6. Horse Guards Building
7. Houses of Parliament & Big Ben
8. Savile Row
9. Tate Britain
10. Westminster Abbey
11. Westminster Cathedral

presented in style. Not to mention all the carriages: the Gold State Coach weighing 4 tons is only brought out on very special occasions. The *Victoria Memorial* in front of the palace gates was erected in memory of the present Queen's great-great-grandmother who made this palace the permanent residence of the royals in 1837. And this is also the spot where the spec-

tacle of the ● *changing of the guard* takes place *(May–July daily 11:30am, Aug–March every other day – except when it rains | www.changing-guard. com)*. A regiment of the royal infantry *(Queen's Foot Guards)* proceeds from Wellington Barracks to Buckingham Palace, accompanied by rousing marching music. *Tube Victoria: Green Park*

▣ CHURCHILL WAR ROOMS
(142 A2) (∅ J7)

Map room, gas masks, microphone for the speeches: in Winston Churchill's underground command centre during the Second World War time stood still on 16 August 1945. Follow the life story of the great statesman (1874–1965), who was both Prime Minister and Minister of Defence between 1940 and 1945. *Daily 9:30am–6pm | £17.25 (incl. audioguide), £19 incl. donation | Clive Steps | King Charles St. | www.iwm.org.uk/visits/ churchill-war-rooms | tube Circle, District: St James's Park*

▣ DOWNING STREET
(142 A2) (∅ J–K7)

Since 1735, British Prime Ministers have resided in this (blocked-off) side street off Whitehall. Tomcat Larry, the "Chief Mouser", who is in charge of dealing with irreverent mice and rats, has been in office longer than any Prime Minister. The Chancellor of the Exchequer lives next door (no. 11). *www.number10.gov.uk | tube Circle, District, Jubilee: Westminster*

▣ HANDEL & HENDRIX HOUSE
(133 D6) (∅ G6)

Jimi Hendrix and George Frideric Handel were neighbours? It's hard to believe but both famous musicians actually lived door to door in Brook Street and rocked London – only 200 years apart. Handel composed some of his best-known work here, e.g. the "Messias" and the "Music for the Royal Fireworks". Letters, sheet music and paintings are exhibited in his former living quarters. Hendrix' success started in swinging London in 1966/67 with "Hey Joe" and "Purple Haze". His flat is as colourful as the wild times he lived in. Regular **INSIDER TIP** events and concerts *(from 6pm | from £5). Museum Mon–Sat 11am– 6pm Sun noon–6pm | £10, online reser-* vation possible *| 25 Brook Street | handel hendrix.org | tube Central, Jubilee: Bond Street*

▣ HORSE GUARDS BUILDING
(142 A2) (∅ K7)

Members of the Queen's Life Guard stand watch with shining helmets and immobile expressions in front of this building, constructed symmetrically around a courtyard. The ● traditional changing of the guard, in which new watchmen come in on horseback *(Mon–Sat 11am, Sun 10am)*, always attracts many on-lookers. Only members of the royal family are allowed to ride through the archway. Discover the *Household Cavalry Museum (www.house holdcavalrymuseum.co.uk)* telling the story of the regiment. You are only a plexiglass screen away from the horses! *Whitehall | tube Charing Cross*

▣ HOUSES OF PARLIAMENT & BIG BEN ★ (142 A3) (∅ K8)

The "mother of all parliaments" is well known from countless postcards, coasters and fridge magnets. But when you see Charles Barry's Victorian neo-Gothic masterpiece with its golden turrets, pinnacles and filigree work for the first time, you will not be disappointed. The imposing *Westminster Hall* dating back to 1099 with its oak hammer-beam roof is the only thing that remains from the medieval *Palace of Westminster*. The bell tower, renamed "Elizabeth Tower'"in 2012 in honour of the Diamond Jubilee, is a symbol of London. The famous 13-ton bell Big Ben has been ringing every hour since 1859. This is where the *House of Commons* (lawmakers) debates take place; their neighbours, the *House of Lords*, are only able to delay laws. Only 90 hereditary lords sit here now (among other memebers), but reform of the upper house remains a bone of contention. The debates of both houses are pub-

An ample abode for the mother of all democracies: the Houses of Parliament with Big Ben

lic; usually, those in the House of Commons are more fun: *Mon 2:30pm–10:30pm, Tue/Wed 11:30am–7:30pm, Thu 9:30am–5:30pm, occasionally Fri 9:30am–3pm.* **INSIDER TIP** On Saturdays and in the summer break both the House of Commons and the House of Lords open their doors; *Mon–Sat 9:15am–4:30pm | £18.50 (incl. audioguide), duration 60–75 min | www.parliament.uk | tube Circle, District, Jubilee: Westminster*

8 SAVILE ROW (133 E6) (*∅ H6*)

Since the mid-19th century, this side street has been considered the finest street in London for gentlemen's tailors. In the late 1960s, Savile Row chose a new image, also dressing pop celebrities like Mick Jagger and the Beatles, who were recording in the same street at the Apple Records Studio (no. 3). Today, one of the most famous addresses for a *sharp suit* is the unconventional *Ozwald Boateng* on the corner of Clifford Street. *www.savilerowbespoke.com | tube Oxford Circus*

9 TATE BRITAIN ⭐ (142 A5) (*∅ J–K9*)

Sir Henry Tate made a fortune with sugar in the 19th century but his real passion was art. He donated his collection to the National Gallery and also paid for half of the proper museum to display it in. The listed building in neoclassical style showcases British art from the 16th century up to today, including the moralistic narrative paintings of William Hogarth, the poetic religious visions of William Blake, the pastoral landscapes of Thomas Gainsborough and John Constable, the nature and feminine mystique of the Pre-Raphaelites and the anthropomorphic sculptures of Henry Moore. Don't miss the Turners in the dedicated *Clore Gallery.* Joseph Mallard William Turner (1775–1851) was a master of the atmospheric interplay of light and colour. Every year from October to early January Tate Britain showcases the work of four artists shortlisted for the important and often controversial *Turner Prize,* awarded in

December. *Daily 10am–6pm | free guided tours daily 11am, noon, 2pm, every first Fri of every second month 6pm–10pm with entertainment | Millbank | www.tate.org.uk | tube Victoria: Pimlico*

🔟 WESTMINSTER ABBEY ★
(142 A3) (*𝌆 K8*)

Coronation church of the royals and sepulchral church of high society. Edward the Confessor started work on building perpendicular style. 3,300 famous Brits lie buried here: scientists such as Isaac Newton and Charles Darwin, composers like Henry Purcell and George Frederic Handel, and politicians such as William Pitt the Younger and W E Gladstone. In *Poets' Corner* look for the graves of Geoffrey Chaucer (Canterbury Tales, 1400) and Charles Dickens. Many others are commemorated by memorial plaques. In 1637, playwright Ben Jonson

Westminster Abbey, coronation church of English kings: a view of the main altar

the church but died a week after its consecration. Edward's successor William the Conqueror was crowned king here on Christmas Day 1066.

Of the original structure currently only the Norman undercroft is open to the public. The Gothic nave of the "new" (13th-century) building is filled with over 600 monuments, plaques and tomb slabs. The *Henry VII Chapel* from the early 16th century boasts a spectacular fan-vault in the had himself buried standing up, to save money! Outside, the two towers were added in 1745 by Christopher Wren's pupil Nicholas Hawksmoor (1661–1736). In 1953, over 8,000 people followed the coronation of Elizabeth II live; in 2011, 2.5 billion people were glued to their TV screens for Will & Kate. Arrive early, or take part in a weekday ● **INSIDER TIP** evensong service *(5pm, Sat/Sun 3pm | free admission). Mon, Tue, Thu, Fri*

9:30am–3:30pm, Wed until 6pm, Sat until 1:30pm, Sun for services only | £20, guided tours (book in advance) £5, free audioguide, also as a download | tel. 72225152 | 20 Dean's Yard | www.west minster-abbey.org | tube Circle, District, Jubilee: Westminster

11 WESTMINSTER CATHEDRAL ●
(141 E4) *(m H9)*

Spectacular neo-Byzantine church with campanile sporting bands of red brick and white stone. The interior of the cathedral serving the Roman Catholic minority religion, begun in 1895, is a work in progress: marble and mosaic tiles grow up the red-brick walls. Don't miss the *Holy Souls* chapel in the northern aisle, where over 100 types of marble were used, the canopy on yellow marble pillars above the high altar, and the bas-relief Stations of the Cross by Eric Gill (1918). An elevator *(Mon–Fri 9:30am–5pm, Sat/Sun until 6pm | £6)* whisks you up to the 🔎 viewing platform. *Mon–Fri 7am–5:30pm, Sat/Sun 8am–6pm | 42 Frances St. | www.westminstercathedral. org.uk | tube Victoria*

BLOOMS-BURY/COVENT GARDEN/ SOHO

As a buffer between the centre of power of Westminster and the money machine of the City, Covent Garden and Soho are in charge of fun and shopping. Here in the cosmopolitan West End, theatres, musicals and multiplex cinemas mix with many alternative shops as well as the big labels.

The name "Soho" is derived from a hunting call; in modern times, the royal hunting grounds became the district of peepshows and by-the-hour hotels. The sex industry is still present, but today Soho mainly caters to broader entertainment needs, and particularly around Old Compton Street is a parade ground for the gay scene. Let a rickshaw pull you through the party scrum and explore the shops, restaurants and pagoda-style archways of Chinatown along Gerrard and Lisle Streets. Soho is also where the heart of the British creative industries beats: film producers in hip outfits, advertising people and design consultants chat about scripts and filming schedules at cramped tables, often served by hopeful acting students.

Literary-minded folk will want to stroll through Bloomsbury to the north, with pleasing streets full of blue memorial plaques for illustrious former inhabitants and green squares serving pretty Georgian residences. Russell Square is the largest square in London. At the western end, look out for the green Victorian taxi drivers' snack shack, a listed *cabman's shelter* serving discount-priced tea and sandwiches to cab drivers – and tourists if you ask nicely. In this district between the two World Wars the literary circle of the Bloomsbury Group formed around Virginia Woolf, John Maynard Keynes, E. M. Forster and others. Here, you find the cultural temple of the British Museum next to antiquarian booksellers and the University of London. On the northern rim, towards King's Cross, the city is being transformed with many new buildings and new use of space.

1 ALL SAINTS (133 E5) *(m H5)*

In striking contrast to the Buddhist Fo Guang Shan Temple diagonally opposite: the church with the most extravagant interior design in London. The geometric mosaics, colourful tiles, playful columns and clouds of incense are an expression of Anglo-Catholic High Church style. *Daily 7:30am–7pm | 7 Margaret St. | www.allsaintsmargaretstreet.org.uk | tube Bakerloo, Central, Victoria: Oxford Circus*

▌2▐ BRITISH LIBRARY
(134 A1–2) (*J–K 2–3*)

The national library receives a copy of every book published in Great Britain; with over 170 million works, the 1997 building – controversial at the time for its slightly brutalist brick architecture – is already bursting at the seams. Amongst the spaces open to the public are the *Sir John Ritblat Gallery (free admission)* with valuable manuscripts including the 8th-century Lindisfarne Gospels, the Magna Carta of 1215 and Beatles song lyrics scribbled out in their handwriting. *Mon, Fri 9:30am–6pm, Tue–Thu 9:30am–8pm, Sat 9:30am–5pm, Sun 11am–5pm | 96 Euston Road | www.bl.uk | tube King's Cross/St Pancras*

▌3▐ BRITISH MUSEUM ★ ●
(134 A4) (*J–K4*)

The world-famous national museum is London's most popular attraction. The building's *Greek Revival* style is beautifully complemented inside by Norman Foster's glass-roofed *Great Court (Sat–Thu 9am-6pm, Fri 9am–8:30pm)*. The largest glass-covered interior in Europe encloses the dome of the famous Reading Room, where Karl Marx wrote his bestseller *Das Kapital*.

If you're on limited time, the best thing to do is to concentrate on the highlights: the treasures of the *Sutton Hoo* ship burial of the Anglo-Saxon tribal ruler Redwald (7th century), the *Lewis* chess figures (12th century), the *Lindow Man* bog mummy or the Egyptian *Rosetta*

Norman Foster's ambitious glass roof spans the Great Court of the British Museum

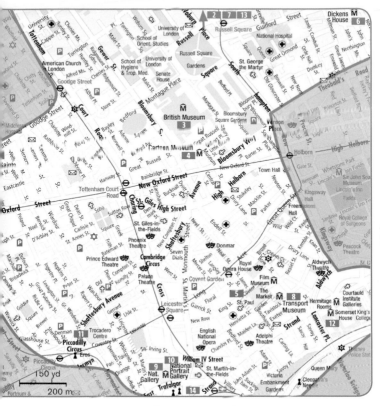

SIGHTSEEING IN BLOOMSBURY/COVENT GARDEN/SOHO

- **1** All Saints
- **2** British Library
- **3** British Museum
- **4** Cartoon Museum
- **5** Covent Garden Piazza
- **6** Dickens' House
- **7** King's Cross Station
- **8** London's Transport Museum
- **9** National Gallery
- **10** National Portrait Gallery
- **11** Piccadilly Circus
- **12** Somerset House
- **13** St Pancras
- **14** Trafalgar Square

Stone hieroglyphs. Still unresolved is the issue of the *Elgin Marbles*, marble statues, horseback sculptures and friezes dating back to the 5th century before Christ, which were shipped – or rather stolen – by Lord Elgin in the early 19th century from the Parthenon to England and are forever being claimed for return to Athens. *Mon–Thu, Sat/Sun 10am –5.30pm, Fri 10am–8:30pm | free admission | multimedia guide £5 | "Eye Opener" tours and lunchtime lectures Tue–Fri 1:15pm free of charge, Fri evening spotlight tours | Great Russell St. | www.thebritishmuseum.ac. uk | tube Central, Northern: Tottenham Court Road*

4 CARTOON MUSEUM
(134 A4) (*CD* K5)

It was the Brits who invented the cartoon as a work of art, and in 2006 the country's first cartoon museum opened. Read a few pages of "The Beano", the comic that many Londoners grew up with. Changing exhibitions, fun greeting cards for sale. *Tue–Sun 10:30am–5:30pm, Sun noon–5:30pm | £7 | 35 Little Russell Street | www.cartoonmuseum.org | tube Central, Northern: Tottenham Court Road*

5 COVENT GARDEN PIAZZA
(134 A6) (*CD* K6)

At weekends in particular, more tourists than Londoners rendezvous here, but the streets around the old fruit and vegetable market are great for shopping, strolling and people watching. St Paul's is the actors' church, featuring memorials for Charlie Chaplin and Boris Karloff. *Tube Piccadilly: Covent Garden*

6 DICKENS' HOUSE
(134 B3) (*CD* L4)

Charles Dickens' (1812–70) Victorian bestsellers helped to create the image of London of that time in and outside England, and it was in this house that the novelist wrote "Oliver Twist" and "Nicholas Nickleby". Exhibits on view include letters, manuscripts and his writing desk. Tours and special events are offered on several days every year, e.g. on the night of Halloween *(£15, reserve in advance!)*. *Tue–Sun 10am–5pm | £9 | 48 Doughty St. | www.dickens museum.com | tube Central: Chancery Lane; Piccadilly: Russell Square*

7 KING'S CROSS STATION
(134 A1) (*CD* K2)

"The next train will depart from platform $9^3/_4$!" The installation in the main hall showing a luggage trolley disappearing into the wall references Harry Potter and the Hogwarts Express. But even without this highlight the main hall of this centrally located railway station *(www.kingscross.co.uk)* is quite spectacular: a network of white steel braces supports a semi-circular glass roof. North of the station is *Granary Square*, pulsating with urban and student life after recent reconstruction measures and lots of cafés and events right next to Regent's Canal. *St Martins College of Art & Design* and the culture complex *King's Place (www.kingsplace.co.uk)* are also close by. *Tube King's Cross/St Pancras*

8 LONDON'S TRANSPORT MUSEUM
(134 B6) (*CD* K6)

This fascinating museum asks the question how Londoners have got around over the course of the past centuries. Exhibits

LOW BUDGET

So much in London is free. The websites *www.whatsfreeinlondon.co.uk*, *www.freetoursbyfoot.com* and *www.londonforfree.net* list guided tours, festivals, exhibitions, open days and cultural events costing nothing or £4 at the most.

Tourist attractions often offer online savings, as well as options to combine two attractions and save: e.g. London Eye with sightseeing cruise on the river or church visits with concerts.

In summer, look out for the *More London Free Festival's* films, music and theatre on the Thames free of charge *(www.morelondon.com/events/calendar)*.

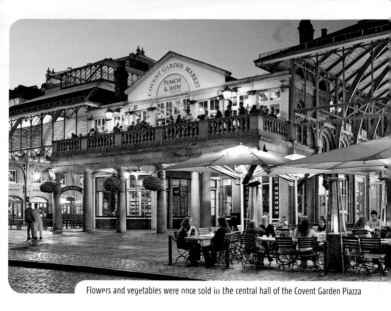

Flowers and vegetables were once sold in the central hall of the Covent Garden Piazza

range from horse-drawn carriages via the first tube train to future transportation systems. Fun and imaginative souvenirs for sale in the gift shop. *Sat–Thu 10am–6pm, Fri 11am–6pm | £17 (children under 18 free) | 39 Wellington St. | www.ll museum.co.uk | tube Piccadilly: Covent Garden*

9 NATIONAL GALLERY ★
(142 A1) *(ﬄ J6)*

The imposing building with the pillared portico on Trafalgar Square was completed in 1838. Today, it shelters one of the world's most important collections of European Old Masters (1250–1900). Don't miss Jan Van Eyck's "The Arnolfini Wedding", John Constable's "The Hay Wain" and Raphael's "Madonna of the Pinks" (1507/08). At the INSIDER TIP long museum night on Fridays there is live music with additional guided tours and talks. *Sat–Thu 10am–6pm, Fri 10am–9pm | daily free guided tours 11:30am,*

2:30pm | free admission | Trafalgar Square | www.nationalgallery.org.uk | tube Bakerloo, Northern: Charing Cross

10 NATIONAL PORTRAIT GALLERY ●
(142 A1) *(ﬄ J6)*

What an entertaining way to approach British history: portraits spanning five centuries, from the Tudor Queen Elizabeth I and the only known likeness of William Shakespeare to the current portraits of the Queen and other VIPs. For fabulous views across Trafalgar Square, Whitehall and Houses of Parliament, visit the ≈ *Portrait Restaurant*. Audiovisual guide with recordings from Churchill to Florence Nightingale £3. Theme apps for iPhone £0–3. Fri from 6:30pm INSIDER TIP Drop-in drawing workshop. *Mon–Wed, Sat/Sun 10am–6pm, Thu/Fri until 9pm | free admission | 2 St Martin's Place | www. npg.org.uk | tube Bakerloo, Northern: Charing Cross*

⓫ PICCADILLY CIRCUS
(133 F6) (*ᗰ J6*)

Traditional meeting place under huge neon advertising hoardings. The slim Eros statue at its centre was put up in 1892 to commemorate the charitable deeds of Lord Shaftesbury; the angel with arrow symbolises Christian charity. *Tube Bakerloo, Piccadilly: Piccadilly Circus*

⓬ SOMERSET HOUSE
(134 B6) (*ᗰ L6*)

Fascinating ensemble of museums on the bank of the Thames with pleasant terrace café and often (free) events in the court-yard: cooling fountains in summer, London's most romantic ice rink in winter. In the summer there are open-air concerts and movie showings and exhibitions and events take place throughout the year. The *Courtauld Gallery* offers an outstanding art collection (Impressionists, 20th century), the *Embankment Galleries* has changing exhibitions with views of the Thames. *Daily 10am–6pm | from £7 | Strand | www.somersethouse.org.uk, courtauld.ac.uk/gallery | tube Circle, District: Temple or Embankment*

⓭ ST PANCRAS (134 A1–2) (*ᗰ K2*)

George Gilbert Scott's grandiose neo-Gothic *Midland Grand Hotel* (closed in 1935, reopened in 2011 as *Renaissance St Pancras Hotel*), a late Victorian brick building with terracotta bands, topped with pointed arches and turrets, oriel windows and chimney pots in front of St Pancras train station, is endowed with a breathtaking façade. This is where the *Eurostar* train arrives, only 30 minutes after leaving the Channel tunnel at Folkestone. The 9 m/30 ft-high bronze statue of a kissing couple towers under the famous railway clock. There are cafés, boutiques and Europe's longest champagne bar – how about a classy

sparkling rosé wine from the south of England? *www.stpancras.com | tube King's Cross/St Pancras*

⓮ TRAFALGAR SQUARE
(142 A1) (*ᗰ J–K6*)

With *Nelson's Column* rising up nearly 165 ft above the lion-guarded fountain and equestrian statues, this is the true heart of London. A bronze plaque at the statue of Charles I on horseback on the southern side of the square marks the geographical centre of London. Trafalgar Square bears the name of the sea battle against a French-Spanish fleet in which Admiral Nelson was victorious but lost his life. *St Martin-in-the-Fields church (Mon, Tue, Thu, Fri 8:30am–1pm, 2pm–6pm, Wed 8:30am–1:15pm, 2pm–5pm, Sat 9:30am–6pm, Sun 3:30am–7pm | www.stmartin-in-the-fields.org)* offers ● free lunchtime concerts *(Mon, Tue, Fri 1pm)*. Free of charge as well: the temporary exhibitions of contemporary art in the INSIDER TIP *Café in the Crypt* and on Wed jazz night. *Tube Bakerloo, Northern: Charing Cross*

CITY/CLER-KENWELL/HOLBORN

It was in the City of London, the "Square Mile", that the city's history began some 2,000 years ago – as the Roman outpost Londinium.

The big banks in the City currently handle a huge proportion of global and European financial transactions. But its future as a major financial centre is in grave doubt as Brexit negotiations continue. If access to the European domestic market is lost, the whole district is likely

Popular meeting place: no chance for solitude at Piccadilly Circus

to undergo substantial change. It has already had to deal with massive losses as it is – both financial and reputational – from the financial crisis of 2008, to the government's austerity measures and the scandal surrounding rigged reference interest rates. From Monday to Friday you feel the pulse of the business world on the streets. In the evenings and at weekends, however, the City becomes a ghost town. The skyline of the City is changing all the time; a number of old churches peek out between the office towers; one that is hard to miss is of course St Paul's Cathedral, the emblem of the city. The architect of St Paul's, Sir Christopher Wren (1632–1723), left his mark on the City like no other. After the Great Fire of 1666 he designed over 50 City churches, amongst them St Stephen Walbrook and St Mary-le-Bow; the reconstruction marked the birth of modern London. The

eastern edge of the City has been revitalised over the past few years by artists and tie-wearing folk looking for cheap space to live and work. It's a similar story west of the City, where in the former printers and jewellery quarter of *Clerkenwell* trendy clubs and bars, designers and restaurants have set up shop. And south of the old media mile of Fleet Street, around the Inns of Court of *Holborn,* is the domain of the British justice apparatus, the rambling courtyards and flawless lawns of the Inner and Middle Temple, narrow alleyways and Victorian pubs providing an insight into London of the 18th century.

■ BANK OF ENGLAND MUSEUM
(135 E5) *(ᗰ N5)*

Play currency broker, examine banknotes or lift a gold bar. This elegant museum tells the story of the national bank, shows

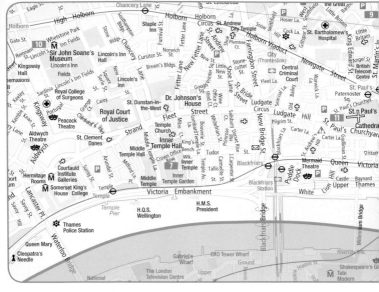

SIGHTSEEING IN CITY/CLERKENWELL/HOLBORN

1 Bank of England Museum
2 Bevis Marks Synagoge
3 Bunhill Fields
4 Guildhall
5 Heron Tower
6 Skyscrapers in the City

every British note that was ever in circulation, as well as clever fakes. *Mon–Fri 10am–5pm | free admission | Bartholomew Lane | www.bankofengland.co.uk/museum | tube Bank*

2 BEVIS MARKS SYNAGOGUE
(136 B5) (🗺 P5)

The oldest synagogue in the country was built in 1701 by Sephardic Jews from Spain and Portugal fleeing the Inquisition. Queen Victoria's Prime Minister Benjamin Disraeli (1804–81) worshipped here until converting to Anglicanism at the age of 12. Join a guided tour and hear the story behind the seven chandeliers and the wooden benches dating back to the time of Oliver Cromwell, and why one seat always remains cordoned off. Nearby the

good kosher *Bevis Marks restaurant (Mon–Fri noon–3pm, Mon–Thu 5:30pm–10:30pm | 3 Middlesex St. | tel. 72 47 54 74 | www.bevismarkstherestaurant.com | Moderate).* Synagogue: *Mon, Wed/Thu 10:30am–2pm, Tue, Fri 10:30am–1pm, Sun 10:30am–12:30pm, closed on Jewish holidays | £5 | guided tours: Wed, Fri 11:45am, Sun 10:45am | Bevis Marks | www.bevismarks.org.uk | tube Liverpool St*

3 BUNHILL FIELDS
(135 F3) (🗺 O3–4)

Green oasis popular for lunch breaks. The mass grave for the victims of London's plague epidemics *(bone hill)* was never consecrated however. Thus, up to the closure of the cemetery in the 19th century it was mainly religious non-

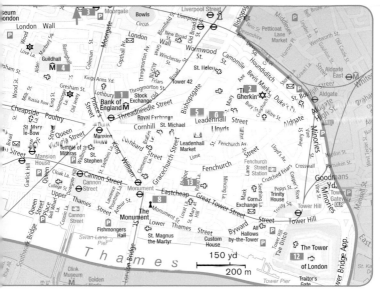

conformists such as Quakers and Methodists who found their last resting place here: for instance the poet and painter William Blake (1757–1827) and the author of "Robinson Crusoe", Daniel Defoe (1661–1731). *April–Sept Mon–Fri 8am–7pm, Oct–March until 4pm, Sat/Sun 9:30am–4pm, in summer until 7pm, guided tours April–Oct Wed 12:30pm | start: Attendant's Hut in the garden | £8 | www.cityoflondon.gov.uk | 38 City Road | tube Northern: Old Street*

4 GUILDHALL (135 F5) (*Ø N–O5*)

"Domine dirige nos" (Lord, guide us), the City's motto, has pride of place above the main entrance to the City of London's official administrative HQ since the 12th century. The pretty, never crowded art gallery displays a representative selection of London scenes, and the medieval crypt displays the fascinating and cleverly illuminated remains of the Roman amphitheatre. *Mon–Sat 10am–5pm, Sun noon–4pm | free admission | Tue, Fri/Sat 12:15pm, 1:15pm, 2:15pm, 3:15pm 45 minute free guided tour to the highlights | Guildhall Yard | Gresham St. | www.guildhall.cityof london.gov.uk | tube Moorgate*

5 HERON TOWER ✻ (136 A5) (*Ø P5*)

A fear of heights is not recommended as you ascend to the 40th floor of the *Heron Tower* by glass elevator. If you have reserved a table at the *Duck and Waffle (daily | duckandwaffle.com | Moderate–Expensive)* you can enjoy a view that makes London look like a playground for builders. And judging by all the construction cranes, there's still a lot more to come. *110 Bishopsgate | tube Metropolitan: Liverpool Street*

■6 SKYSCRAPERS IN THE CITY
(136 A–B5) (∅ P5)

What are a gherkin and a shard doing in the City? Those are the nicknames of two of the most conspicuous architectural structures among the many glittering skyscrapers in this area. Norman Foster's 180 m/551 ft high *Gherkin*, officially called *Swiss Re Building (30 St Mary Axe)*, was erected in 2004 on the site of the *Baltic Exchange* building that was destroyed by the IRA. The tower is not open to visitors but the *Konditor & Cook Café (Mon–Fri 7:30am–6pm | entrance at the back | www.konditorandcook.com)* serves sweet and savoury treats to office workers and tourists alike. The *Shard* right across the street, built in 2014, is officially the *Leadenhall Building (122 Leadenhall Street)* (225 m/738 ft). This tower can also only be admired from the outside. Turn around and you will be facing the *Lloyd's Building (1 Lime Street/corner of Leadenhall Street)*. In 1986 architect Richard Rogers applied the futuristic style principles of the Centre Pompidou in Paris to the headquarters of the trad-ition-steeped insurance company and turned it "inside out" by placing pipes, exhaust system, ventilation shafts and elevators on the outside. At night the building is illuminated in blue and could easily be part of the film set of "Blade Runner". *Tube Circle, District: Monument or Metropolitan: Aldgate/Liverpool Street*

■7 INNS OF COURT
(134 B–C 4–6) (∅ L5)

It was around the four Inns of Court that English *common law* developed in medieval times; today the gabled halls, alleyways and lawns of this training institution of the legal elite have kept a timeless aura and provide a stylish picnicking space. Any specialised *barristers* (as opposed to *solicitors*) belong to one of the Inns and have to have taken at least 12 dinners there! The 15th-century *Old Hall of Lincoln's Inn* survived World War II undamaged, *Temple Church (138 C5) (∅ L5) (admission £5 | www.templechurch.com)* (1185) is London's only remaining round church. Wed at 1:15pm often INSIDER TIP free organ recitals. Explore on a weekday to catch the atmosphere. *Tube Central: Holborn*

■8 MONUMENT ↘ (135 F6) (∅ O6)

The world's tallest freestanding stone column offers fabulous views indeed.

FIT IN THE CITY

Explore London with guided *jogging tours (tel. 0845 5 44 04 33 | www.cityjoggingtours.co.uk)*: along the river, through the parks, in Greenwich or Hampstead (6–12 km/3–6 miles). Learn to kayak in the *Shadwell Basin (Glamis Road | 74 81 42 10 | www.shadwell-basin.org.uk | train DLR: Shadwell)*, a former harbour basin. Is there more? Yes: yoga for free but only for early birds: Tue 7.30am free yoga lesson in the church *St. Stephan with St. John Westminster (Rochester Row | www.sswsj.org | tube District, Circle: Victoria)*.

The futuristic skyline of London's City including the Gherkin and the Shard

Designed in 1666 by Christopher Wren to commemorate the Great Fire of London, laid out flat it would stretch 62 m to the bakery in Pudding Lane where the fire started. At the exit you are given a certificate that you have successfully completed the 311 steps. *Daily 9:30am–5:30pm, in summer until 6pm | £4 | Fish St | www.themonument.info | tube District, Circle: Monument*

9 MUSEUM OF LONDON ★
(135 E4) (*M N4–5*)

Once upon a time the Romans founded the city of Londinium. Later the Anglo-Saxons conquered it as Lundenburgh. The Black Death and the Great Fire of London left their mark on it, as did Queen Victoria. But this museum tells no fairytales: this is history brought to life. Stir an Anglo-Saxon cooking pot, learn which type of street food was popular in the Middle Ages, stroll through a **INSIDER TIP** Victorian shopping street

complete with hairdresser, toilet and pub or a *Pleasure Garden*. Not to mention the golden carriage of the Lord Mayor. After all these artefacts and multimedia impressions, stop outside to take a look at a piece of the *London Wall*, a remnant of the city's former fortifications. *Daily 10am–6pm | free admission | London Wall | www.museumoflondon.org.uk | tube Circle, Hammersmith & City, Metropolitan: Barbican*

10 **INSIDER TIP** SIR JOHN SOANE'S MUSEUM ● (134 B5) (*M L5*)

A residence with squeaking floorboards, full to the ceiling with sculptures, antiquities, medals and curiosities, this treasure trove is the result of the passion for collecting of Sir John Soane (1753–1837). The son of a bricklayer and architect of the Bank of England mandated that after his death nothing should be changed. But the curators didn't always adhere to his wishes. After a long period of renovation many rooms have now been converted back to their original state so you can experience how the Soanes slept and what their bathroom looked like. Admire the architectural models in the studio, an Egyptian sarcophagus, William Hogarth's "The Rake's Progress" morality cycle, as well as architectural drawings. *Tue–Sat 10am–5pm, guided tours Tue, Sat 11am, Tue, Thu–Sat noon (£10), every first Tue of the month 6pm–9pm candle-light tour (expect long queues!) | free admission | 13 Lincoln's Inn Fields | www.soane.org | tube Central, Piccadilly: Holborn*

11 ST PAUL'S CATHEDRAL ★
(135 E5) (*N5*)

A church dedicated to Saint Paul has been standing here since 604, and when the predecessor of the current building, the huge Gothic Old St Paul's, burnt down in 1666, the moment had come for Christopher Wren's masterpiece. The capstone was placed in 1711, during the reign of Queen Anne, whose statue in front of the imposing western façade flanked by Baroque twin towers curiously turns its back on St Paul's. In World War II St Paul's enormous lead-covered dome amid the smoke and flames of the aerial bombardment became a symbol for Londoners' determination and resistance. The crypt shelters the tombs of the British heroes the Duke of Wellington and Admiral Lord Nelson.

Starting from the southern aisle walk up to the dome, past trompe-l'œil frescoes. If you whisper something into the walls of the *Whispering Gallery* people on the opposite side, over 30 m away, can hear you – in theory, because you won't be the only ones to try this.

From the uppermost ◆ *Golden Gallery* you have a fantastic view over the city. Attending *Choral Evensong (Mon–Sat 5pm, Sun 3:15pm)* is free for worshippers.

Mon–Sat 8:30am–4pm | £18, online £16 (incl. multimedia guide and tours), note: large bags are not allowed inside! | Sun services only | guided tours 10am, 11am, 1pm and 2pm | www.stpauls.co.uk | tube Central: St Paul's

12 TOWER OF LONDON ★
(144 B1) (*P6*)

The place where London began is a fascinating complex with 900 years of history as a royal residence, prison, arms depot, mint and safe for the Crown Jewels. The centrepiece of the Unesco World Heritage site is the *White Tower*, begun in 1076, at the time of William the Conqueror; here you can see armour worn by Henry VIII and the Norman *Chapel of St John* (1080), the oldest sacred building in London still standing. Illustrious prisoners such as Sir Walter Raleigh and Lady Jane Grey were brought into the Tower from the Thames, through *Traitors' Gate*.

The *Bloody Tower* was used by the infamous Duke of Gloucester, the future Richard III, to imprison his two nephews, 10 and 12 years of age: "for their own safety". Whether he actually had them murdered here, too, is only one of the Tower's mysteries. In the *Jewel Tower* a conveyor belt carries you swiftly past the Crown Jewels, including the crown of the late Queen Mum with the Koh-i-Noor diamond and the huge *Punch Bowl* (235 kg). Arrive early before too many tour groups manage to distract from the historic charm of the Tower, and join a *Beefeater* tour (every 30 min.).

The traditionally privileged Tower guards were joined in 2007 by a woman. The wings of the ravens are clipped, as legend has it that if the ravens leave the tower, the monarchy will fall. A monument commemorates those executed in the Tower – the last a German spy in 1941. *March–Oct Tue–Sat 9am–5:30pm, Sun/Mon from*

The Tower of London is on all tour groups' to-do list

10am, Nov–Feb Tue–Sat 9am–4:30pm, Sun/Mon 10am–4:30pm | £22.50, online £21 | audioguide £4 | www.hrp.org.uk | tube Circle, District: Tower Hill

🔢 20 FENCHURCH STREET 🔆 (136 A6) (𝕞 O6)

The block towering up between Fenchurch Street and Eastcheap is sure to grab your attention. *20 Fenchurch Street* (160 m/525 ft), designed by Rafael Viñoly, quickly acquired a fitting nickname: "Walkie-Talkie". With a free ticket (which can only be booked in advance!) you can enter the building and ride up to the **INSIDER TIP** *Skygarden (skygardentickets. com)* with its tropical greenery. All that's left to do now is press your nose against the glass and gape: Wow, what a view! *20 Fenchurch Street | tube Circle, District: Monument*

SOUTH BANK & SOUTH-WARK/ BANKSIDE/ LAMBETH

The poor south versus the rich north? This dichotomy doesn't quite hold up anymore. The south bank of the Thames is gradually shedding it's poverty-stricken image and now boasts enough attractions to hold its own against the north side of the river.

When you stroll along the south bank of the river today, stopping for a coffee or a pint, taking a spin in the London

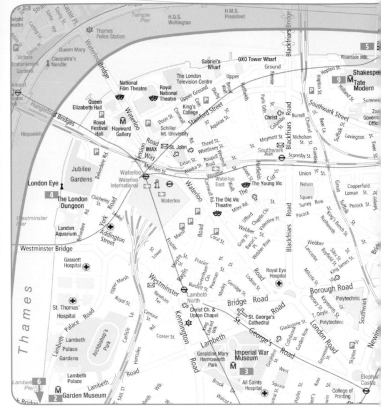

SIGHTSEEING IN SOUTH BANK & SOUTHWARK/BANKSIDE/LAMBETH

1 City Hall/GLA

2 Garden Museum

3 Imperial War Museum

4 London Eye

5 Millennium Bridge

6 MI 6 Building

Eye or enjoying contemporary art in the Tate Modern, it is hard to imagine that this was once considered the poor side of London.

In Shakespeare's time it was a place of gambling and prostitution. Later it was an industrial area and in the 1950s cultural institutions were housed here – all of them looking longingly towards the well-to-do north bank, with its wealth

of imposing buildings including the seat of government, the Houses of Parliament. But things all changed at the turn of the 21st century: Shakespeare's Globe Theatre was brought back to life and the Bankside Power Station was converted into the Tate Modern. Architectural highlights such as the Millennium Bridge, the London Eye, the Sea Life Aquarium and the spectacular Shard skyscraper

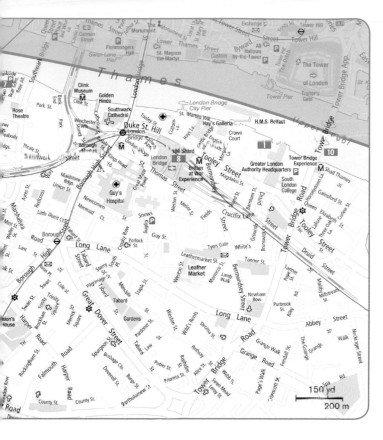

7 Shakespeare's Globe Theatre **9** Tate Modern
8 The Shard **10** Tower Bridge

soon followed and designer offices, galleries, cafés, pubs and restaurants started popping up everywhere. The south bank became a shopping and party area. Gentrification is also progressing in residential districts south of the river such as Bermondsey, where trendy locations and new shops and boutiques seem to suddenly appear all the time. The flip side to this development: social housing buildings from the 1970s are being torn down to make way for exclusive tower blocks which the current inhabitants, predominantly on lower incomes, can no longer afford.

1 CITY HALL/GLA ✪ (144 B1) (⌖ P7)
The seat of the Greater London Authority (GLA), London's city government, is literally askew. Norman Foster's vaguely egg-

shaped glass building leans away from the Thames and thanks to an eco cooling system only uses a quarter of the energy of a normal office building of this size. *Mon–Thu 8:30am–6pm, Fri until 5:30pm | The Queen's Walk | www.london.gov.uk | tube Jubilee, Northern: London Bridge*

2 GARDEN MUSEUM (142 B4) *(K9)*

Prehistoric agricultural tools, old watering cans and wheelbarrows: St Mary-at-Lambeth church displays tools used by John Tradescant the Elder and John Tradescant the Younger, a father-and-son team of royal gardeners and plant collectors in the 16th/17th century who are also buried in the church grounds. A part of the museum exhibition is dedicated to them and the surrounding gardens show examples of their gardening art. The pretty café beckons visitors in need of a little break. *For prices and opening hours see: www.gardenmuseum.org.uk | Lambeth Palace Road | tube Bakerloo: Lambeth North*

3 IMPERIAL WAR MUSEUM (146 C4) *(M8–9)*

The cannons in the garden are pointed towards the entrance gate and remind visitors what a terrible thing war is. Nevertheless the museum has all kinds of military equipment on display: Spitfires and biplanes hang from the roof of the atrium designed by Norman Foster; T34 tanks, V2 rockets and army vehicles are testimonials of two devastating world wars. In other galleries the human face of war – including a portrayal of the life of soldiers and life during World War II air raids – as well as famous military manoeuvres such as the D-Day landings are conveyed spectacularly using special effects. *Daily 10am–6pm | free admission | Lambeth Road | www.iwm.org.uk | tube Bakerloo: Lambeth North*

4 LONDON EYE ★ ● (142 B2) *(K–L7)*

London's best attraction by a mile, unless you suffer from vertigo! Europe's tallest observation wheel (443 ft) stands on the bank of the Thames. The view from the glass pods, holding 25 passengers each, is unbeatable; on a clear day you can see for miles, in the evenings drift romantically above the lights of the city. Extra: a *4 D Experience* film shown before you board, with live wind and weather effects. Stylish version: on the INSIDER TIP Gin& Tonic Ride you get to sip cocktails and go around twice (£39.95). *Sept–March daily 10am–8:30pm, April–Aug 10am–9pm, Fri/Sat until 9:30pm, closed two weeks in Jan | £24.95 (£21.20 online) | tel. 087 17 81 30 00 (*) | www.londoneye.com | tube Circle, District: Waterloo, Westminster*

If you're not frightened of heights: fantastic views from the London Eye

⑤ MILLENNIUM BRIDGE
(135 E6) (*∅ N6*)

The first new bridge to be built across the Thames for over a hundred years connects two London icons: St Paul's Cathedral and the Tate Modern. The inspiration behind the 325 m-long filigree steel footbridge, designed by Norman Foster and sculptor Anthony Caro, was a beam of light. Shortly after its inauguration in 2000 it turned out that the structure couldn't cope with the number of visitors: the bridge started moving from one side to the other. It cost £5 million to install a new buffering system. *Tube Central: St Paul's; Circle, District: Blackfriars*

⑥ MI 6 BUILDING (142 A6) (*∅ K10*)

This postmodern building will probably look familiar to James Bond fans: in "Skyfall" (2012) it was spectacularly blown up and in "Spectre" (2015) it was still in a state of decay. Of course, all espionage experts know that this (in films as in real life) is the headquarters of the British Secret Intelligence Service MI6. *85 Albert Embankment | tube Victoria: Vauxhall*

⑦ SHAKESPEARE'S GLOBE THEATRE
(143 E1) (*∅ N6*)

This is where William Shakespeare hung out in the late 16th century. His plays were performed in the octagonal open-air theatre until it burned down. In the late 1990s the theatre was reconstructed on its original site so all Shakespeare fans can now enjoy a play out in the fresh air, visit the exhibition *(Mon–Sun 9am–5pm)* or go on a guided tour *(Mon, 9:30am–*

5pm, Tue–Sat 9:30am–12.30pm, Sun until 11.30am, every 30 min. | £15 | no umbrellas, no cameras! Closed during afternoon performances | For more information: tel. 79 02 15 00). Performances in the *Sam Wanamaker Playhouse* are illuminated by candles. *Late April–early Oct Mon–Sat 2pm, 7:30pm, Sun 1pm, 6:30pm | £5–10 (standing tickets) to £62 | 21 New Globe Walk | tel. 74 01 99 19 | www.shakespearesglobe.com | tube Circle, District: Mansion House; Northern, Jubilee, trains: London Bridge*

8 THE SHARD ● ⅍
(143 F1) (*ω O7*)

Opened in 2012, The Shard, measuring 310 m/117 ft and built on the south bank of the Thames, stretches into the Lon-

The Shard: London's new landmark is recognisable from everywhere

don skyline and has become a new landmark. Visitors can take the high-speed lift to the viewing platform of the office building and enjoy a 360° view. Magnificent! Why not celebrate with a nice **INSIDER TIP** glass of champagne *(ticket bought in advance: £33.95). April–Oct daily 9am–10pm, Nov–March Sun–Wed 10am–7pm, Thu–Sat 10am–10pm; book ahead; bag size is limited! | £30.95, bought in advance: £29.95, incl. audioguide | St Thomas Street | tel. 0844 4 99 71 11 (*) | www.theviewfromtheshard.com | tube Northern, Jubilee: London Bridge*

9 TATE MODERN ★
(143 E1) (*ω N6*)

The largest museum in the world for contemporary art is the brightest star among London's museums. Since its opening in 2000 the huge brick edifice has caused a stir with daring installations and projects in the turbine hall by the likes of Anish Kapoor, Louise Bourgeois or Ai Weiwei. The Swiss architects Herzog & de Meuron who originally converted the former power station into a museum have now also designed the new pyramid shaped annex Switch House. In the lower tanks of the building the smell of oil still lingers. The annex not only gives the museum 60 per cent more space but also a ⅍ **INSIDER TIP** breathtaking view from the 10th floor. Espresso bars, café, restaurant; multimedia guide, mobile app. *Sun–Thu 10am–6pm, Fri/Sat 10am–10pm | free admission | free guided tour of the highlights daily 11am, noon, 2, 3pm | 53 Bankside | www.tate.org.uk | tube Jubilee: Southwark; Circle, District: Blackfriars; Central: St Paul's*

10 TOWER BRIDGE ★
(144 B1) (*ω P–Q 6–7*)

Alongside Big Ben, the neo-Gothic twin towers (1894) of Tower Bridge are the most famous symbol of London. The

Tower Bridge Exhibition (access from the northern tower) leads you into the Victorian engineering room with the original steam engines; enjoy an unusual and very photogenic view over the Thames from the ✅ glassed-in pedestrian walkways. *April–Sept daily 10am–5:30pm, Oct–March 9:30am–5pm | £9 | www.towerbridge.org.uk | tube Circle, District: Tower Hill*

MORE SIGHTS

CAMDEN (0) (*₥ G–H1*)
Listen to the alternative heartbeat of the city in this north London borough, to the tune of rock, psychedelic, punk and electro sounds. Discover the market, clubs, bars, contemporary theatre, dance and performances, but also the INSIDER TIP *Jewish Museum (Sat–Thu 10am–5pm, Fri until 2pm | £7.50 | www.jewishmuseum. org.uk)*, which tells the story of the British Jewish community and the worldwide diaspora and explains Jewish rituals. Café. *www.camdentown.co.uk | tube Northern: Camden*

GREENWICH ★ (0) (*₥ 0*)
Here in the heart of British maritime culture in the southeast of the city, London gets its dose of sea air. Best take a whole day to discover this Unesco World Heritage Site. Near the last tea clipper Cutty Sark *(www.rmg.co.uk)* look out for the domed entrance to a pedestrian tunnel under the Thames. At the *Old Royal Naval College (www.ornc.org)* admire the Baroque symbolism of the ceiling paintings in the *Painted Hall* and the ornate chapel opposite, and wander uphill between the ancient trees of London's most beautiful park, past the *National Maritime Museum (www.rmg.co.uk)* with Captain Cook's sextants, Titanic memorabilia and the

world's largest collection of maritime art. The world sets its watches by Greenwich Mean Time, and on the prime meridian in front of the *Royal Observatory (daily 10am–5pm | £9.50, or as a combined ticket including a boat ride from £22.50)* you can stand with one leg in the western and the other in the eastern hemisphere. The bronze cone of the ● *Planetarium (sky shows at variable times | £7)* bends at an angle towards the polar star. ✅ From the top of the hill you have a fantastic view of the Docklands with *Canary Wharf*. The impressive office compound with the three high buildings is London's answer to Manhattan. *Tube Greenwich, DLR: Cutty Sark*

HAMPSTEAD (0) (*₥ 0*)
This pleasant slice of village London with its arty and exclusive atmosphere has a pretty High Street and with the extensive landscaped park of ● *Hampstead Heath*, the green lung of north London, a playground for walkers, dog owners and kite fliers. From ✅ *Parliament Hill* you get a fabulous sweeping view across the city. *Tube Northern: Hampstead*

HAMPTON COURT PALACE (0) (*₥ 0*)
Henry VIII who is known for his six wives – and for getting rid of them one after the other – lived here. His Cardinal, Thomas Wolsey, had built the palace in 1520 but was forced to leave after he fell from grace because he could not convince the Pope to grant Henry a divorce from Catherine of Aragon. Henry then had the palace converted and enlarged for his wives and court. The brick edifice with turrets and ornamental chimneys grew considerably and is now considered one of the most important remaining examples of fine Tudor architecture. Allow for at least three hours to take in all the sights including the

Great Hall, the Tudor kitchen area, the exhibition on Henry's childhood days, his private rooms and the extensive gardens. *April–Oct daily 10am–6pm, Nov–March until 4:30pm | £19 (incl. audioguide), online £18 | East Molesey, Surrey | www.hrp.org.uk | trains: Hampton Court (from Waterloo)*

HIGHGATE CEMETERY
(0) (*꘭ 0*)

London's most famous cemetery was recently immortalised in Audrey Niffenegger's novel "Her Fearful Symmetry" (2009); twisted paths lead past overgrown tombs with dramatic funerary sculptures. Karl Marx (1818–83) spent half of his life in London. Instead of the simple tomb that he had wished for, there's a bearded sphinx-like bronze bust with the inscription "Workers of all Lands unite". Punk designer Malcolm McLaren is buried here too. *April–Oct Mon–Fri 10am–5pm, Sat/Sun 11am–5pm, Nov–March until 4pm | £4.* The **INSIDER TIP** western, spookier part of the cemetery with its Gothic tomb sculptures and mausoleums can only be visited on a guided tour. Highlights are the *Egyptian Avenue* and the *Circle of Lebanon Vaults:* catacomb tombs in the shade of an imposing Lebanese cedar. This part inspired Bram Stoker's novel "Dracula". *Guided tours (70 min) March–Nov Mon–Fri 1:45pm (book well in advance!), all year round Sat/Sun every 30 min 11am–4pm | ticket sales from 10:45am | £12 | Swains Lane | tel. 83 40 18 34 | highgatecemetery.org | tube Northern: Archway*

KEW GARDENS ★
(0) (*꘭ 0*)

Palm trees, water lilies, tropical water plants and even corals apparently feel very much at home in the gigantic Victorian greenhouses. 250 years of the art of gardening are exhibited in the Royal Botanical Gardens. Almost every plant on earth grows here thanks to specially emulated climatic conditions. Take a guided tour through the treetops 18 m/59 ft off the ground on the *Treetop Walkway (1 hour, daily 11am, noon, 1:30pm, register 15 min. in advance)* or ride more comfortably on the *Kew Explorer* train *(£5)*. The ticket also gives you access to *Kew Palace (April–Sept daily 10:30am–5:30pm)*. *Kew Gardens: daily from 10am, variable closing times from 4:15am to 7:30pm | £16 | Kew Road | www.kew.org | tube District: Kew Gardens | in summer by boat from Westminster to Kew (April–Oct | £13 | 90 min.)*

MADAME TUSSAUDS ★
(132 C3) (*꘭ F4*)

Do you want to feel like a star and walk the red carpet alongside Kate Winslet or Brad Pitt? Hug George Clooney and hang out with JLo? Or meet and greet model Cara Delevingne and super athlete Usain Bolt? Madame Tussauds' wax museum makes everyone's star struck dreams come true! *Daily 9:30am–5:30pm (longer in summer) | £35 with queuing, £29 online, children under 14 must be accompanied by a grown-up | Marylebone Road | www.madametusauds.com/london | tube Baker Street*

MUSEUM OF LONDON DOCKLANDS
(0) (*꘭ 0*)

In a former warehouse for sugar, coffee and rum in the shadow of the office towers of Canary Wharf, this engaging museum tells the story of 2000 years of Thames shipping and also dedicates one gallery to Great Britain's less than glorious role in the transatlantic slave trade. *Daily 10am–6pm | free admission | West India Quay | www.museumoflondon.org.uk/museum-london-docklands | tube*

Notting Hill is full of small exceptional and sometimes decidedly weird shops

Jubilee: Canary Wharf; DIR: West India Quay

NOTTING HILL
(130 A–C4–6) (*m* A–B 5–6)

Blame it on Julia Roberts and Hugh Grant and their "Notting Hill" movie: originally housing many Caribbean immigrants, Notting Hill has changed beyond recognition. The pretty colourful houses – small shops, cafés and gastropubs – are worth millions, and the area is in danger of falling victim to its own trendy image. *Tube Central: Notting Hill Gate*

QUEEN ELIZABETH OLYMPIC PARK ●
(147 D3) (*m* 0)

The Olympic grounds of 2012 have been turned into an attractive park with a lot of space to relax, including playgrounds and picnic spots. Among the remnants from the Olympics are the *Aquatics Centre,* the *Stadium,* the *Velopark* and the 115 m/377 ft high intricately constructed steel sculpture ≈ *Arcelor Mittal Orbit (April–Sept daily 10am–6pm, Oct–March*

11am–5pm | tickets exclusively online, just view £10, with slide £15 | tickets. arcelormittalorbit.com).* Enjoy the view over London from one of the platforms or rush down through the tunnel slide. You can also cross the Thames in ≈ cable cars that were specially designed for the Olympic Games (between North Greenwich and Royal Victoria Docks). Shopping fans will have a great time in *Westfield Stratford City Center. queenelizabetholympicpark.co.uk | tube Central, Jubilee: Stratford*

SHERLOCK HOLMES MUSEUM
(132 B3) (*m* F4)

With actor Benedict Cumberbatch taking on the role, Sherlock Holmes, one of the best-known literary figures of all times has been transported into the 21st century. His house at no. 221B Baker Street doesn't actually exist but the museum at no. 239 takes great pains to recreate the home of the famous detective. Take a picture sitting in the armchair with hat and pipe before you tour the rest of the house. *Daily 9.30am–6 pm | £15 | 239 Baker Street | www.sherlock-holmes.co.uk | tube Baker Street*

SHRI SWAMINARAYAN MANDIR (NEASDEN TEMPLE)
(0) (🛱 0)

2,000 tons of Carrara marble and 2,800 tons of Bulgarian limestone twirl up to the skies in filigree domes and turrets; inside, flower-bedecked altars celebrate Hindu deities (murtis). This magnificent Mandir temple, the largest outside India was built in the early 1990s by a Hindu sect. *Hinduism Museum (£2)*, good vegetarian cuisine in the attached INSIDER TIP *Shayona Restaurant (daily | tel. 89 65 33 65 | www.shayonarestaurants.com | Budget). Daily 9am–6pm | 105–119 Brentfield Road | londonmandir.baps.org | tube Harlesden (Bakerloo), then bus 224*

SPITALFIELDS
(136 B/C 4) (🛱 P/Q 4)

The original fruit and veg market was relocated in the 1990s. Since then a vibrant creative scene has popped up around the halls of *Spitalfields Market* (see p. 79) with vintage clothing stores as well as art and crafts shops. Young designers move here looking for cheap studios to rent. *www.spitalfields.co.uk | tube Liverpool Street*

THAMES FLOOD BARRIER
(0) (🛱 0)

In an emergency, the gates of the high-tech flood barrier (1982), cased in huge steel-coated engine rooms, can rise up from the riverbed and close London off from the tides. The best view is from Thames Barrier Park. *(North side Thames, DLR: Pontoon Dock)*. The visit can be combined with a short detour to *Trinity Buoy Wharf (daily 9am–5pm | www.trinity buoywharf.com | DLR: East India)*, a for-

mer materials warehouse for Thames buoys which was converted into a space for artists' studios made out of containers. A small information centre on the south bank demonstrates how the flood barrier works. *Nov–March Thu–Sun 11am–3:30pm, April–Oct Thu–Sun 10:30am–5pm | £4 | 1 Unity Way | tube North Greenwich (then bus 472)*

WIMBLEDON LAWN TENNIS MUSEUM (0) (🛱 0)

The museum all about the time-honoured tennis tournament presents the history of the sport, original trophies such as dresses worn by the Williams sisters, videos of the big matches and also memorabilia of the Olympic Games of 2012. *Daily (except during tournament time) 10am–5pm | £13, £24 with 1.5-hour guided tour | Church Road | Wimbledon | guided tours: tel. 89 46 61 31 | www.wimbledon.com | tube District: Southfields, then bus 39*

TRIP

WINDSOR CASTLE & ETON COLLEGE (146 B4) (*∅ 0*)

Windsor Castle (March–Oct usually daily 9:30am–5:30pm, Nov–Feb 9:45am–4:15pm | £20 incl. audioguide | www. royal collection.org.uk), the Queen's "weekend cottage", is perhaps even slightly grander than her city palace. On a tour lasting two to three hours you wander through the *State Rooms (open all year)* and *Semi-State Rooms (Oct–March)* furnished with splendid antiques and paintings by Rembrandt, Rubens and Canaletto. Don't miss the 1 m/3 ft high pretty Queen Mary's Doll House with its miniature furnishings: real books, lifts and furniture just like in a proper palace.

Ten monarchs lie buried in *St George's Chapel*, the chapel of the Order of the Garter. The changing of the guard can be witnessed April–July Mon–Sat 11am, otherwise alternating monthly on even-numbered days and odd-numbered days. *Train from Waterloo or Paddington or Greenline bus no. 701, 702*

If you get hungry you will have to inter-rupt your visit and grab a bite to eat in one of the numerous cafés in the vicin-ity of the castle as the Queen doesn't like the smell of greasy chips. Eton Col-lege, the school that makes Prime Minis-ters (it has spawned 19 to date), is about 15 minutes walking distance away. It was founded in 1440 for poor but gifted stu-dents and is regarded as one of the most exclusive schools in the world today. On a guided tour you will get to see the old-est still existing classroom and learn just how tough education was in the 15th century. *Closed for visitors at the time of print, enquire about guided tours | www. etoncollege.com*

The Queen's carriage in front of Windsor Castle

FOOD & DRINK

British food has long ceased to be good for a cheap laugh; today, London boasts over 50 Michelin-starred eateries and fulfils all culinary desires: from Afghan to Zen food, via kosher-Chinese, garlic cuisine and gluten-free fare all the way to food as experience. And the sushi and tapas fever continues too.

Under the flag of modern British, modern European or Asian fusion, London chefs bring exciting, if sometimes a bit over-the-top creations on to the table. Meanwhile, many Londoners have turned into amateur chefs, inspired by TV chefs such as the down-to-earth Delia Smith, laid-back Jamie Oliver or the sensual Nigella Lawson. It's only at weekends that Londoners would go to the trouble of making a classic English breakfast. During the week,

functional *caffs* offer super-cheap mugs of tea, *baked beans* in tomato sauce on toast, fried eggs and sausages. *Caffs* are a part of British working-class culture and in homage to the high percentage of deep-fried fare are also sometimes called *greasy spoons*. More and more en vogue are *organic* and *fair trade* products, while porridge has made a comeback. In recent times, the cup of tea or *cuppa* has been widely supplanted by milky coffees *(latte/ flat white)*. You'll find a Starbucks at every corner in London.

Britons only take a short break for lunch; a sandwich at their desk often has to suffice. They have several words to describe the evening meal: tea is taken between 5.30pm and 7pm while supper is a light evening meal and dinner is the more for-

Photo: Afternoon tea – stylish at The Ritz

A culinary journey of discovery through the continents and satisfying all palates: from *greasy spoons* to destination restaurants

mal option. A London favourite and also a late-night staple to soak up too many pints of beer, are Indian restaurants, more often than not in fact run by Bangladeshis. Chinatown has *all-you-can-eat* buffets for under £10. Recommended chain restaurants are *Prezzo (www.prezzorestaurants. co.uk)* and *Wagamama* (Japanese, *www. wagamama.com)*. Especially at weekends, you should book a table in advance. The website *www.toptable.co.uk* is a useful tool for online table reservations and often has special offers. Restaurants usually serve lunch from noon to 3pm and dinner from 6 to 11pm (earlier on a Sunday). Many restaurants offer the option of a *pre-theatre meal* between 5:30 and 7pm.

AFTERNOON TEA

Once at least, treat yourself to a traditional *afternoon tea* in a fancy hotel: mini sandwiches with cucumber, salmon or egg, scones with clotted cream and jam, and patisseries. Adding a glass of champagne is becoming ever more popular.

Maison Bertaux patisseries – winning the hearts of Londoners

108 PANTRY (132 C4–5) (*ID G5*)

Finally even people with gluten intolerance can enjoy their afternoon tea! The *Marylebone Hotel* serves buttermilk scones, cake and pastries – gluten free or classic – in a bright and friendly interior. *Daily noon–5pm | from £28 | 108 Marylebone Lane | tel. 79 69 39 00 | 108brasserie.com | tube Central, Jubilee: Bond Street*

PALM COURT
(133 D4) (*ID H5*)

The restaurant in the *Langham Hotel* has already received the Tea Council award for the best afternoon tea in London. Mini sandwiches and scones are served with tea, as well as authentic sweets and exquisite tartlets. *Afternoon tea (from £49) daily 1pm, 3:15pm, 5:30pm | 1 C Portland Place, Regent St. | tel. 79 65 01 95 | www. palm-court.co.uk | tube Oxford Circus*

POSTCARD TEAS ● (133 D5) (*ID G5*)

Worship at the altar of the English national drink in the Japanese-inspired teashop run by the former art dealer Timothy d'Offay. A fun touch: post your favourite tea to loved ones back home. Tea classes *(Sat 10am)* are also available. *Mon–Sat 10:30am–6:30pm | 9 Dering St./New Bond St. | tel. 76 29 36 54 | www. postcardteas.com | tube Oxford Circus*

THE RITZ ★ (141 E1) (*ID H7*)

● Tea at the *Palm Court* of the *Ritz* is a society ritual worth sharing. £52 gets you the city's finest tea, sandwiches, scones, patisseries. For gentlemen, a jacket and tie are obligatory: no jeans or trainers! Booking essential. *Daily 11:30am, 1:30pm, 3:30pm, 5:30pm, 7:30pm | 150 Piccadilly | tel. 73 00 23 45 | www.theritzlondon. com | tube Jubilee, Piccadilly, Victoria: Green Park*

CAFÉS

INSIDER TIP ATTENDANT
(133 E4) (*ID H5*)

Quite an unusual location for a café: a former (!) Victorian men's urinal. The ceramic tiles have remained and account for the charming atmosphere. *Mon–Fri 8am–6pm, Sat/Sun 10am–5pm | 27a Foley Street | the-attendant.com | tube Northern, Central: Goodge Street, Oxford Circus*

DRINK, SHOP & DO
(134 B1) (*ØØ K2*)

Trendy vintage café-cum-shop that runs crafts workshops and dance classes. Everything you see is for sale: crockery, tea towels, old-fashioned sweeties. Fri/Sat from 7pm dancefloor (free entry until 10pm). **INSIDER TIP** Sunday *bottomless-brunch* with prosecco and vegan delights (book in advance). *Mon–Thu 10:30am–midnight, Fri, Sat until 2am, Sun until 8pm | 9 Caledonian Road | tel. 72 78 43 35 | www.drinkshopdo.co.uk | tube King's Cross*

LOOK MUM NO HANDS!
(135 E3) (*ØØ N4*)

Even if you didn't crash your bike when you let go of the handlebars, you can still sip your coffee at one of the large wooden tables in this bike repair café. They also serve sweet and savoury food. *Mon–Fri 7:30am–10pm, Sat/Sun from 9:30 am | 49 Old Street | tel. 72 53 10 25 | www.lookmumnohands.com | tube Circle, Nothern: Barbican, Old Street*

MAISON BERTAUX
(133 F5) (*ØØ J5*)

Legendary croissants and delicious pastries in this timeless Soho institution (since 1871!). *Daily from 9am | 28 Greek St. | www.maisonbertaux.com | tube Northern, Piccadilly: Leicester Square; Central, Northern: Tottenham Court Road*

NOTES
(134 A6) (*ØØ K6*)

Finest coffee beans from the coffee shop's own roastery, brewed in the stylish es-

presso machine or retro-style using a porcelain filter: a civilised cup of the finest coffee is served here accompanied with porridge or toast with avocado. *Mon–Fri 7:30am–9pm, Sat 9am–10pm, Sun 10am–6pm | 31 St Martin's Lane | tel. 72 40 04 24 | www.notes-uk.co.uk | tube Bakerloo, Northern: Charing Cross; Northern, Piccadilly: Leicester Square*

BRITISH

BOISDALE OF BELGRAVIA ★
(141 D4) (*ØØ G9*)

Gourmets will love this: a Scottish influenced menu including lobster, salmon and haggis. And for desert there's **INSIDER TIP** whisky and a big Havana cigar. Live jazz music tops off the experience. *Mon–Fri noon–1pm, Sat from 6pm |*

MARCO POLO HIGHLIGHTS

★ **The Ritz**
Tea time in one of London's top hotels → p. 64

★ **Boisdale of Belgravia**
Scottisch menu plus live jazz music → p. 65

★ **Inn the Park**
Breakfast and more in a green setting with pond view → p. 66

★ **Dishoom**
Yummy Indian food with a special flair → p. 66

★ **Sardo**
Authentic Sardinian cuisine in Bloomsbury → p. 69

★ **The Palomar**
New interpretations of Israeli cuisine → p. 71

15 Eccleston Street | tel. 77 30 69 22 | www.boisdale.co.uk | tube Circle, Victoria: Victoria | Moderate–Expensive

HAWKSMOOR GUILDHALL
(134 F5) (*ᗙ N–O5*)

Lovers of great meat portions will love this steakhouse. Beneath art deco lamps you can sumptuously dine – starting with an English breakfast. *Mon–Fri 7am–10am, noon–3pm, 5pm–10:30pm | 10 Basinghall St. | tel. 73 97 81 20 | www.thehawksmoor.com | tube Bank, St Paul's, Moorgate | Moderate–Expensive*

INN THE PARK ★
(141 F2) (*ᗙ J7*)

Airy wood-panelled stylish restaurant overlooking the pond in St James's Park. It serves delicious food from breakfast to afternoon tea (book in advance). How about trying Cornish crabs with avocado for lunch? *Mon–Fri 8am–11am, noon–9pm, Sat/Sun from 9am | tel. 74 51 99 99 | tube Bakerloo, Northern: Charing Cross | Moderate*

PETRUS (140 C3) (*ᗙ F8*)

This Michelin-starred restaurant under the helm of Gordon Ramsay is the

FAVOURITE EATERIES

Pizza pilgrimage

After a few beers two brothers decided to quit their jobs and start baking pizza full time. Seeing that they didn't know the first thing about it, they travelled to Italy to learn the trade and came chugging back to London in a Piaggio Ape. They installed a big pizza oven in the tiny three-wheeled car and lo presto! *Pizza Pilgrims* **(133 E–F 5–6)** *(ᗙ J5–6) (Tue–Fri noon–3pm | pizza pilgrims.co.uk/the-van | tube Central, Northern: Tottenham Court Road | Budget)* was born. You can find them on Berwick Street Market *(www.ber wickstreetlondon.co.uk/the-market)*.

Sweet on the road

Enjoy your afternoon tea with sandwiches and scones during a 90-minute tour of the city on the Routemaster bus past Big Ben, Buckingham Palace and Hyde Park. Book the tour with the INSIDER TIP B Bakery Bus *(from £45, prices vary depending on seat, day and*

time | tel. 30 26 11 88 | b-bakery.com/ afternoon-tea/afternoon-tea-bus-tour) in advance. It starts at 8 Northumberland Av. **(142 A1)** *(ᗙ K7) (tube Bakerloo, Northern: Charing Cross) daily 12:30pm and 3pm* or Victoria Coach Station **(141 D5)** *(ᗙ G9) (tube Circle, District: Victoria) daily noon, 2:30pm, 5pm, Fri–Sun also 1 and 3.30pm.*

Bombay feeling

Buzzing ceiling fans, dimmed lights: the atmosphere of the Irani Mumbai café ★ *Dishoom* **(136 B2–3)** *(ᗙ P3) (Mon–Fri 8am–11pm, Sat/Sun from 9am | 7 Boundary Street | tel. 4 20 93 24 | www.dishoom.com/shoreditch | tube Overground: Shoreditch High Street | Budget–Moderate)* is as heart warming as the delicious Indian menu which includes tandoori grilled dishes, biryanis and a British-Indian breakfast (they even have a gluten free one!). Enjoy your meal out on the beautiful colonial style veranda.

attempt to counter criticism that the top chef has his fingers in too many pies. Modern French cuisine in art deco ambience. If money's no object, book a place at the Chef's Table – right inside the kitchen! *Mon–Sat noon–2:15pm, 6:30pm–10:15pm Sun until 9:30pm | 1 Kinnerton Street | tel. 75 92 16 09 | www.gordonramsay.com | tube Piccadilly: Knightsbridge | Expensive*

POPPIES
(136 B–C4) (*∅ Q4*)

Long before this quarter became trendy, Pop Newland supplied the East End with sound ● fish & chips. The fish comes in fresh from Billingsgate Market. *Daily 11am–11pm | 6–8 Hanbury St. | tel. 72 47 08 92 | www.poppiesfishandchips.co.uk | tube Northern: Liverpool St., Old St. | Budget*

ROAST (143 F1) (*∅ O6*)

There's no better place for traditional British food than the Floral Hall at Borough Market. Early birds can have kippers (smoked fish) and kedgeree (rice with fish) for breakfast. And how about roast beef with Yorkshire pudding for lunch? *Mon–Fri 7am–3.45pm, 5:30pm–10:45pm, Sat 8:30am–3:45pm, 6pm–10:45pm, Sun 11:30am–6:30pm | Stoney Street | tel. 30 06 G1 11 | www.roast-restaurant.com | tube London Bridge | Moderate*

ROCK & SOLE PLAICE (134 A5) (*∅ K5*)

London's oldest *chippie* has been frying fish & chips since 1871. Also takeaway. *Daily noon–11pm | 47 Endell St. | tube Piccadilly: Covent Garden | Moderate*

RULES (134 A6) (*∅ K6*)

London's oldest restaurant (since 1798), famous for its game and salmon dishes, has something of an old country house:

Rules: London's oldest restaurant

wooden panelling, heavy curtains, velvet coverings, with paintings, prints and hunting trophies on the walls. Online reservation for up to 6 people. *Mon–Sat noon–11:45pm, Sun until 10:45pm | 35 Maiden Lane | tel. 78 36 53 14 | www.rules.co.uk | tube Piccadilly: Covent Garden | Moderate*

INSIDER TIP THE SHED ☺
(138 C1–2) (*∅ B7*)

A rural-rustic ambience meets you in *The Shed,* a restaurant run by three brothers who take their ingredients from their family farm in West Sussex to create authentic dishes. *Tue–Sat noon–3pm, 6pm–11pm | 122 Palace Gardens Terrace | tel. 72 29 40 24 | www.theshed-restaurant.com | tube Central: Notting Hill Gate | Budget*

EUROPEAN

SIMPSON'S-IN-THE-STRAND
(134 B6) (*ⓓ K6*)
This traditional establishment has been serving dishes cooked with regional ingredients for over 185 years. Famous guests to have dined here include Charles Dickens. Start your day in this English club with a great British fry-up of Cumberland sausages, bacon, eggs and tomatoes. *Mon–Fri 7:15am–10:30am, Mon–Sat noon–2:45pm, 5:45am–10:30pm, Sun noon–9 pm | 100 Strand | tel. 78 36 91 12 | tube Bakerloo, Northern: Charing Cross | Moderate*

Meaty meals in modern design: St John

ST JOHN (135 D4) (*ⓓ M4*)
A mecca for carnivores and part of the blooming gastro scene on the Smithfield meat market in trendy Clerkenwell. This place specialises in innards: duck hearts, lamb's tongue, kidneys. *Mon–Fri noon–3pm, Mon–Sat 6pm–11pm | 26 St John St. | tel. 72 51 08 84 | www.stjohnrestaurant.com | tube Circle, Hammersmith & City, Metropolitan: Farringdon | Moderate*

EUROPEAN

THE BELVEDERE ✴ (138 B3) (*ⓓ A8*)
Book a table on the terrace balcony and enjoy views of Holland Park with French cuisine. Book ahead! Mon–Fri 2- or 3-course menus du jour £18/28. *Mon–Sat noon–2:30am, 6pm–11pm, Sun noon–3:30pm | Holland Park | Entrance Abbotsbury Rd. | tel. 76 02 12 38 | www.belvedererestaurant.co.uk | tube Central: Holland Park | Moderate*

BISTRO UNION (0) (*ⓓ 0*)
Rustic bistro in Clapham which serves brunch and snacks at the bar and Anglo-American-French cuisine for dinner, e.g. trout with pea salad. *Mon–Sat 9:30am–10pm, Sun 5:30pm–6:30pm | 40 Abbeville Road | tel. 70 42 64 00 | www.bistrounion.co.uk | tube Northern: Clapham South | Budget*

BRASSERIE ZÉDEL
(133 E–F6) (*ⓓ J6*)
Descend into the basement for an authentic Parisian ambience. Excellent French cuisine at extremely reasonable prices. 2-course menus for under £10. Daily live music from 9:30 pm. *Mon–Sat 11:30am–midnight, Sun until 11pm | 20 Sherwood St. | tel. 77 34 48 88 | www.brasseriezedel.com | tube Northern, Bakerloo: Piccadilly Circus | Budget–Moderate*

THE LECTURE ROOM AT SKETCH
(133 E6) (*ⓓ H6*)
This gourmet temple boasts two Michelin stars and delights its guests with a *Gour-*

met *Rapide Lunch* or surprises them with a *Tasting Menu* (also for vegetarians). Book in advance! Lounge on Louis XV chairs in the parlour. *Tue–Fri noon–1:30pm, Tue–Sat 7pm–11pm | 9 Conduit Street | tel. 76 59 45 00 | www. sketch.uk.com | tube Bakerloo, Central, Victoria: Oxford Circus | Expensive*

PRINCI
(133 E–F3) (ᗰ J5)

Italian Restaurant with a modern interior. The wood-burning ovens bake the best pizzas and INSIDER TIP Milan pastries. Good for brunch on Sun (from 11am) and takeaway when it's too crowded. *Daily 8am–11pm | 135 Wardour St. | tel. 74 78 88 88 | www.princi.com | tube Central, Bakerloo, Victoria: Oxford Circus | Budget*

THE REAL GREEK
(134 A5) (ᗰ K5–6)

The name says it all: a lively atmosphere, friendly service, scrumptious food such as lamb cutlets, halloumi cheese spits or good retsina give you the feeling of being in Greece. Right in the heart of London. Reservations recommended. *Mon–Sat noon–11pm, Sun until 10:30pm | 60–62 Long Acre | tel. 72 40 22 92 | www.therealgreek. com | tube Piccadilly: Covent Garden | Budget*

SARDO ★
(133 E3) (ᗰ H4)

This wonderful Sardinian restaurant is suitable both for a romantic evening and for a group booking. Try the *spaghetti bottariga* (sauce made out of roe of the thicklip grey mullet, olive oil), *malloreddus* (durum wheat pasta) or *linguine al granchio* (with crab meat and chili). *Mon–Fri noon–3pm, Mon–Sat 6pm–11pm | 45 Grafton Way | tel. 73 87 25 21 | www.*

sardo-restaurant.com | tube Circle, Hammersmith & City, Metropolitan: Warren St. | *Moderate*

SEVEN PARK PLACE
(141 E1) (ᗰ H7)

The passion for cooking was passed on to William Drabble by his granny. After working in several renowned restaurants in the UK he became the Michelin starred chef of St James's Hotel in 2009 where he creates French dishes with best British ingredients. 2-course lunch menu £26.50. *Tue–Sat noon–2pm, 7pm–10pm | 7–8 Park Place | tel. 73 16 16 15 | www.stjameshotelandclub.com | tube Victoria, Piccadilly, Jubilee: Green Park | Expensive*

INTERNATIONAL

INSIDER TIP BRIXTON VILLAGE MARKET
(0) (ᗰ 0)

Take a culinary trip around the world in the market hall: *Mama Lan* fills hand-

LOW BUDGET

Top restaurants slash their prices at lunchtime; *set meals* are cheaper than à la carte. Look at the "Evening Standard" *(www.standard.co.uk)* and *www.londoneating.co.uk* for good deals.

Comptoir Libanais **(132 C5)** *(ᗰ G5) (daily 8am–10:30pm | 65 Wigmore Street | tel. 79 35 11 10 | www.le comptoir.co.uk | tube Central: Bond Street)* serves tasty Lebanese dishes at acceptable prices. Especially recommended: warm *mezze* for starters and pomegranate lemonade.

LOCAL SPECIALITIES

Ale – heavier dark beer, ideally drunk at cellar temperature, with many regional variations; one local favourite is *London Pride*

Bangers & Mash – sausages and mashed potato. Often to be found in pubs, like *shepherd's pie* (originally a leftover dish) made from mutton or beef mincemeat, covered with a mashed potato crust

Cider – naturally cloudy alcoholic apple drink

Crisps – national potato snack, not to be confused with *chips* (fries)!

Crumpets – round soft yeasty muffin with holes; fabulous toasted with butter

Curry – korma and masala curries are mild, Madras curries rather hot, vindaloo (photo right) is extra hot. Common starters are thin *poppadums* (wafer-thin chickpea-flour crispbread) with *pickles* (onions, mint sauce, chutney); there's also *naan* bread or *chapati* flatbread

Custard – vanilla sauce, often served as an alternative to liquid whipped cream

Fish & Chips – the famous national dish: breaded fish & fries with salt and malt vinegar

Pie – mincemeat in pastry, Victorian fast food

Ploughman's Lunch – a pub-grub staple: bread, butter, cheese, pickles, often served with salad

Roast – a *Sunday roast* – roast beef or roast chicken with roast potatoes and sauce – is served in hotel *carveries* and many (gastro) pubs

Sandwiches – filled with: BLT (bacon, lettuce, tomato; egg & cress; cheese & tomato, prawns ...

Scones – sweet and crumbly; with butter, jam and cream (or even *clotted cream*) they are a firm part of traditional afternoon tea (photo left)

---

made Beijing dumplings with meat and fish. *The Joint* grills chilli-chicken wings served in bread rolls from the *Bad Boy's Bakery*, a social enterprise project. The choice at *Honest Burgers* is simply delicious even for vegetarians. *Okan* serves Japanese street food from Osaka. *Daily from noon | entrance in Coldharbour Lane | www.wearebrixtonvillage.london | tube Victoria: Brixton | Budget*

BUSABA EATHAI
(133 F5) (*ΩΩ J5*)

Relaxed atmosphere if you don't mind that it's a little noisy. *Daily noon–11pm, Sun until 11:30pm | 106–110 Wardour St. |*

tel. 72 55 86 86 | www.busaba.com | tube Bakerloo, Piccadilly: Piccadilly Circus | Budget

HAKKASAN
(133 F5) (ω J5)

Britain's first Michelin-starred Chinese restaurant is slightly hidden away in a side street. Try cod with champagne and honey. Dim Sum Sunday from noon: seasonally inspired 8-course lunchtime menu in the Ling Ling Lounge, from £58 incl. cocktails (min. 2 persons). *Daily noon–3pm, 5:30pm–11:15pm, Thu–Sat until 0:30am | 8 Hanway Place | tel. 79 27 70 00 | www.hakkasan.com | tube Central, Northern: Tottenham Court Road | Expensive*

HUMMUS BROS
(133 F6) (ω J5–6)

A good spot for a fresh and inexpensive Soho snack. The tasty sesame dip forms the basis for various hot and cold toppings, served with warm pita bread.

Daily | 88 Wardour St. | tel. 77 34 13 11 | www.hbros.co.uk | tube Bakerloo, Piccadilly: Piccadilly Circus | Budget

INSIDER TIP ▸ J & A CAFÉ
(135 D3) (ω M4)

Hearty brunch on weekends. Homemade cakes, soups, salads. The entrance lies somewhat hidden off Great Sutton St. *Daily | 4 Sutton Lane | tel. 74 90 20 02 | www.jandacafe.com | tube Circle, Hammersmith & City: Barbican | Budget*

THE PALOMAR ★
(133 F6) (ω J6)

Modern interpretations of Israeli cuisine with North African influences, for example mussels with aniseed or squid with chickpeas. Sit at the bar to watch the chefs at work. *Mon–Sat noon–3:30pm, 5:30pm–11pm, Sun noon–3:30pm, 6pm–9pm | 34 Rupert St. | tel. 74 39 87 77 | www.thepalomar.co.uk | tube Piccadilly, Bakerloo: Piccadilly Circus | Budget–Moderate*

No gaudy Asian decor: Michelin-starred Chinese restaurant Hakkasan

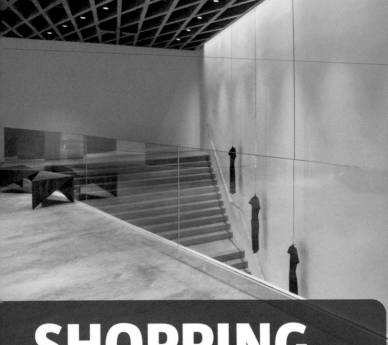

SHOPPING

CITY **WHERE TO START?**
    Oxford Street boasts most of the big department stores (Selfridges, John Lewis, Debenhams), while **Kensington** (Kensington High Street) and **Chelsea** (King's Road) have more class. **Neal's Yard** brings an alternative vibe to the mix. **Carnaby Street** is trendy again; interesting shops can be found around **Brick Lane** too. Overall favourite: **Covent Garden**.

Shopping remains one of the great pleasures of any visit to London, and there's really nothing you can't get here. While London remains expensive, bargains can be had at seasonal sales in early January and July as well as mid-season.

The big stores close around 8pm, on Thursdays often as late as 9pm. Most city-centre shops are open on Sundays from noon to 6pm. One trend are in-store cafés. The Australian department store chain ● *Westfield (www.westfield.com)* has two branches in London, both located in huge shopping malls with approx. 350 stores each: in West London and in Stratford City (East London). At the other end of the scale, look out for quirky *pop-up shops* (temporary outlets, *www. londonpopups.com)*. The chic boutiques for window shopping are on *Bond Street* and *Sloane Street*. Notting Hill has many fun independent shops, as does INSIDER TIP *Redchurch Street* and

Time-honoured traditional stores and the latest fashion trends, markets and delicatessens, antiques and trinkets

INSIDER TIP *Cheshire Street* in the cool East End. Since the 1960s, ★ *King's Road* has been a favourite shopping street for Londoners in the know, while the most famous one is *Oxford Street*. Most department stores are here, with shops from all the leading designers under one roof.

A stone's throw from the madding crowd of Oxford Street, *Marylebone High Street* offers another shopping experience: sophisticated interiors, holistic cosmetics, unusual kitchenware, handbags, children's clothing, books and designer furniture. Unusual shoe shops cluster around *Neal Street* and *Floral Street*. Bookshops can be found in Covent Garden along *Charing Cross Road*, independent music shops in *Berwick Street*. Independent bookstores are located along *Charing Cross Road* and *Cecil Street*. You won't have to look hard for souvenir shops with more or less kitschy knick-knacks. *Cool Britannia (www.coolbritannia.com)* along Whitehall and The Strand stays open until 11pm. For tasteful souvenirs head for the museum shops: art books and prints, cool stationery, umbrellas, etc.

Cath Kidston: pastel tones are back in fashion

ANTIQUES

SILVER VAULTS (134 C4) (𝄞 L5)
Antique silver sold from 30 underground shops, full to the brim with silver spoons, watches, jewellery, napkin rings, vases, candlesticks. *Mon–Fri 9am–5:30pm, Sat 9am–1pm | Chancery House | 53–64 Chancery Lane | www.thesilvervaults.com | tube Central: Chancery Lane*

BOOKS

ANY AMOUNT OF BOOKS
(133 F6) (𝄞 J6)
Extensive old-fashioned second-hand book emporium. *Daily 10:30am to 9:30pm | 56 Charing Cross Road | www.anyamountofbooks.com | tube Northern, Piccadilly: Leicester Square*

DAUNT BOOKS (132 C4) (𝄞 G4)
For a long time now lovers of travel books have been browsing in this beautiful book-shop with long oak galleries under a sky-light. There's also a map and a second-hand section. *Mon–Sat 9am–7:30pm, Sun 11am–6pm | 83 Marylebone High St. | www.dauntbooks.co.uk | tube Central: Bond Street*

FOYLES ● (133 F5) (𝄞 J5)
This independent book temple has successfully managed the transition into modern times. With its 37,000 m² and eight floors the reader's Mecca is bright and airy – despite having 200,000 books on offer! And there is plenty of room for browsing. You can have lunch in the café on the 5th floor or just sip an espresso while surfing the internet. *Mon–Sat 9:30am–9pm, Sun noon–6pm | 107 Charing Cross Road | www.foyles.co.uk | tube Central, Northern: Tottenham Court Road*

GOSH! (133 E–F 5–6) (𝄞 J5–6)
Old and new comic fans will have a blast here: a whole floor dedicated solely to graphic novels! On the ground floor you can browse the latest editions of your favourite comics. *Daily 10:30am–7pm | 1 Berwick Street | www.goshlondon.com | tube Central, Northern: Tottenham Court Road*

GIFTS & ACCESSOIRES

CATH KIDSTON (134 A5) (𝄞 K5)
These Fifties-inspired flower, polka-dot and stripy prints are still the darling of magazine editors. Bags, aprons, tea towels, fabrics, crockery, etc. Several branches. *Mon–Sat 10am–7pm, Sun noon–6pm | 28–32 Shelton Street | www.cathkidston.co.uk | tube Covent Garden*

CERAMICA BLUE (130 A5) (𝄞 O)
French stoneware, Spanish terracotta and fine English china all sitting peacefully side by side: famous chefs like Gordon

Ramsay or Yotam Ottolenghi buy tablewear for their restaurants here. *Mon–Sat 10am–6:30pm, Sun noon–5pm | 10 Blenheim Crescent | www.ceramicablue.co.uk | tube Hammersmith & City: Ladbroke Grove*

CONTEMPORARY APPLIED ARTS
(143 F4) (*ᗰ J5*)

Excellent *crafts,* with a contemporary touch. This community gallery sells individual pieces by 300 top craftspeople and artists: jewellery, metal and woodwork, ceramics, glass, textiles. *Mon–Sat 10am–6pm | 89 Southwark St. | www.caa.org.uk | tube Jubilee: Southwark*

HOPE & GREENWOOD
(134 B6) (*ᗰ K5–6*)

Like the proverbial kid in a sweet shop, rediscover your childhood in this sweet-tooth paradise in Covent Garden; you'll find all the traditional sweets, chocolate buttons, toffees, crumbly cream fudge, liquorice and lots more. *1 Russell St. | www.hopeandgreenwood.co.uk | tube Piccadilly: Covent Garden*

LABOUR & WAIT
(136 B3) (*ᗰ P3*)

An updated version of the traditional *hardware shop.* Tasteful and useful objects and accessories for the home, enticingly presented in a former pub in a hip East End street. Whether mops or workers' outfits, everything has style. *Tue–Fri 11am–7:30pm, Sat/Sun until 6pm | 85 Redchurch St. | www.labourandwait.co.uk | tube Northern: Old Street*

MAIA
(136 C1–2) (*ᗰ Q2–3*)

Unique gold and silver jewellery with colourful semi-precious stones at affordable prices in the form of delicate necklaces, expressive earrings and extravagant rings. High quality standards and ethical principles are also upheld at *Maia's. Sun 10am–5pm (during Columbia Road Flower Markets), often Sat noon–5pm (check in advance) | 118 Columbia Road | www.maia-shop.co.uk | tube Northern: Old Street*

URBANIA
(136 C3) (*ᗰ Q4*)

Unusual handbags, hats, body jewellery, rings and chains: *Urbania* sources its hand-crafted accessories and jewellery from all around the world and sells them for a decent price. *Daily 10am–7pm | 156 Brick Lane | urbiana.co.uk | tube Overground: Shoreditch High Street*

DEPARTMENT STORES

HARRODS ★ (140 B3) (*ᗰ F8*)

At the onset of darkness 12,000 light bulbs illuminate the magnificent ornamental terracotta façade with its green

MARCO POLO HIGHLIGHTS

★ **King's Road**
Shopping street – popular since the Sixties → p. 73

★ **Harrods**
The archetypal department store – go just the once → p. 75

★ **Liberty**
Such pretty fabrics ... A classy shopping experience → p. 76

★ **Fortnum & Mason**
The most English way to go about delicatessen shopping → p. 76

★ **Hotel Chocolat**
Delicate chocolate made from their own cocoa powder → p. 78

★ **Brick Lane Market**
London's trendiest street market → p. 79

marquees. Since it opened in 1849 the famous department store, with 300 departments for fashion, cosmetics, toys, household goods and jewellery, has been an London institution. In the art nouveau food hall with sumptuous wainscot you can find lobster and champagne next to (orange) marmalade and English tea. Watch out, a dress code is in operation: sports shorts, flipflops, cut-off jeans or bare midriffs are taboo, backpacks have to be taken off. *Mon–Sat 10am–9pm, Sun noon–6pm | 87–135 Brompton Road | www.harrods.com | tube Piccadilly: Knightsbridge*

JOHN LEWIS (133 D5) (*Ø G–H5*)
Another traditional institution, this department store has been located in Oxford Street since 1864 but originally only sold curtain fabrics. Today household goods, fashion labels, cosmetics and electronics are displayed on seven floors. Tired of shopping? Then why not take a rest on the beautiful roof terrace (in summer) or one of the restaurants? In 2008 John Lewis was honoured by officially being appointed purveyor to the court of Queen Elizabeth II. *Mon–Sat 9:30am–8pm, Sun noon–6pm | 300 Oxford Street | www.johnlewis.com | tube Central, Victoria: Oxford Circus*

LIBERTY ★ (133 E5) (*Ø H5*)
This stylish department store with the conspicuous Tudor-style timbered façade and stylish open atrium specialises in unusual fabrics, fashions, carpets and accessories. The upper gallery and squeaking stairs were crafted from beams from the last two wooden British warships. The famous Liberty prints (paisley, little flowers, peonies) are available as notebooks, scarves, vanity bags or as fabric by the yard. *Mon–Sat 10am–8pm, Sun noon–6pm | 210–220 Regent St. | www.liberty.co.uk | tube Bakerloo, Central, Piccadilly: Oxford Circus*

SELFRIDGES ● (132 C5) (*Ø G5*)
Only have two hours to go shopping? Selfridges has got to be London's best one-stop shop, with concessions of the most popular designers, fancy cosmetics and food sections – and bright yellow shopping bags. *Mon–Sat 9:30am–9pm, Sun noon–6pm | 400 Oxford St. | www.selfridges.com | tube Jubilee, Central: Bond Street*

LOW BUDGET

Fashion-conscious Londoners browse in *charity shops (www.charityshops. org.uk)* – preferably in wealthy areas such as Chelsea, e.g. at the *British Red Cross (0) (Ø E11) (69 Old Church St. | tube Circle, District: Sloane Square.*

Forever 21 **(132 C5)** *(Ø G5) (Mon–Sat 9am–10pm, Sun noon–6pm | 360 Oxford Street | www.forever21. com | tube Jubilee, Central: Bond Street)* sells low-priced outfits for young people, *Absolute Vintage* **(136 B–C4)** *(Ø P–Q5) (daily 11am–7pm | www.absolutevintage.co.uk | tube Overground: Shoreditch High Street)* specialises in cheap, vintage-style clothes.

CLASSICS
FORTNUM & MASON ★
(141 E1) (*Ø H6*)
Wonderfully eccentric, very English since 1707 – the window decorations alone are works of art! The main tourist magnet is

Selfridges: wide selection of cool designer wear all in one store

the famous delicatessen section with marble columns and chandeliers. Purveyor of fine foods to the royal family since 1814. Fashion, accessories, gifts, and, of course, a splendid afternoon tea. *Mon–Sat 10am–9pm, Sun noon–6pm | 181 Piccadilly | www.fortnumandmason. co.uk | tube Bakerloo, Piccadilly: Piccadilly Circus*

JAMES SMITH & SONS
(134 A5) (*Ø K5*)

There is the odd occasion when an umbrella comes in handy in London. Founded in 1830, this family concern sells umbrellas from micro models to large parasols, plus unusual walking sticks and more. *Mon–Fri 10am–5:45pm, Sat until 5:15pm | 53 New Oxford St. | www.james-smith.co.uk | tube Central, Northern: Tottenham Court Road*

COSMETICS

JO MALONE (140 B4) (*Ø F9*)

Exclusive trendy perfumery with their own perfume collection, with individually put-together skincare lines. *Mon/Tue, Sat 9:30am–6pm, Wed–Fri until 7pm, Sun 11am–5pm | 150 Sloane St. | www.jo malone.co.uk | tube Circle, District: Sloane Square*

NEAL'S YARD REMEDIES ✪
(134 A5) (*Ø K5*)

Established over thirty years ago, purveyor of high-quality organic cosmetics with aromatherapeutic claims. The products contain exclusively natural ingredients and are not tested on animals. New: practical small travel sizes to try out the products. While there are now several branches all over London, the original (and always busy) shop is here in Covent Garden. *Mon–Sat 10am–8pm, Sun until 6:30pm | 15 Neal's Yard | www.nealsyard remedies.com | tube Piccadilly: Covent Garden; Central, Piccadilly: Holborn, then short walk; the branch in Covent Garden is always crowded.*

PENHALIGON'S (141 E1) (*Ø H7*)

Traditional perfume house, founded around 1860 by Barbier Penhaligon, Queen Victoria's perfumer. Soaps and their own perfumes, famous: "Bluebell".

Mon–Sat 10am–6pm, Sun until 5:30pm | 132 King's Road | www.penhaligons.com | tube Circle, District: Sloane Square

Borough Market: popular for its English farmhouse cheese

CULINARY DELIGHTS

ALGERIAN COFFEE STORES
(133 F6) (*00 J5–6*)
A Soho institution for over 130 years now, with 80 kinds of coffee, from regular organic Bolivian and the famous Jamaica Blue Mountain to the world's most expensive gourmet coffee, which passes the digestive tracts of a cat before being roasted, plus 120 blends of tea, in a cosy ambience. Accessories for making coffee and tea and speciality sweets round up the range of products on offer. *Mon–Wed/Sat 9am–7pm, Thu–Fri until 9pm* | 52 Old Compton St. | www.algcoffee.

co.uk | tube Northern, Piccadilly: Leicester Square

HARDYS ORIGINAL SWEETSHOP
(134 A6) (*00 K6*)
Anybody entering *Hardys* will invariably feel like a "kid in a sweetshop". The paradise for people with a sweet tooth sells traditional sweets, chocolate buttons, creamy fudge and liquorice. *Mon–Sat 11am–8pm, Sun 11am–6pm* | 25 New Row | www.hardyssweets.co.uk | tube Piccadilly: Leicester Square

HOTEL CHOCOLAT ★ (134 A5) (*00 K5*)
Find your favourite among the many fine chocolate creations, e.g. the massive *Giant Slabs*, and then treat yourself to a lovely (and not too sweet) hot chocolate in the café section of the shop. The company has its own cocoa plantation in the Caribbean. 25 branches in London. *Mon–Fri 8am–8pm, Sat 10am–8pm, Sun noon–7pm* / 163 Kensington High St. | tel. 79 38 21 44 | www.hotel chocolat.co.uk | tube Circle, District: High Street Kensington

TWININGS (134 C5) (*00 L5*)
Tea has been sold in this narrow wood-panelled shop for 300 years: today, there are dozens of varieties. The selection packs with various interesting flavours and pick-n-mix tea bags make great little gifts. You can sample tea at the tea bar and admire the glass cases displaying Twinings history while sipping. *Mon–Fri 9:30am–7pm, Sat/Sun 10am–5pm* | 216 Strand | www.twinings.co.uk | tube Circle, District: Temple

FASHION

AGENT PROVOCATEUR (133 E5) (*00 J5*)
Satin, ribbons, naughty embroideries: provider of sexy underwear for glamour

girls. *Mon–Sat 11am–7pm, Sun noon–7pm | 6 Broadwick St. | www.agentprovocateur.com | tube Bakerloo, Central, Victoria: Oxford Circus*

COLLECTIF

(136 B–C4) *(Q5)*

Lovers of vintage fashion will strike it lucky here. The dresses and blouses are made of polka dot and flowered pattern with a style mix of the 40s and 50s. Why not grab a matching jacket or bag too? Rockabilly and modern design are all affordable. *Daily 10am–6pm | 58 Commercial Street | www.collectif.co.uk | tube Piccadilly: Covent Garden*

DOVER STREET MARKET

(141 F1) *(I6)*

Beautiful chaos is the slogan of this hip shopping concept, designed by Rei Kawakubo, the Japanese head of *Comme des Garçons*: designer fashion displayed artily across five storeys in Mayfair. *Mon–Sat 11am–7pm, Sun noon–6pm | 18–22 Haymarket | www.doverstreetmarket.com | tube Bakerloo, Piccadilly: Piccadilly Circus*

ORLA KIELY (140 A6) *(E10)*

Irish designer Orla Kiely used to create hats. Alongside her design work for well-known labels she now creates fashion, handbags, kitchen utensils and many more items for her own boutiques. Typical: sixties charm and leafy prints. Prince William's wife Kate is among her customers. *Mon–Sat 10am–6:30pm, Sun noon–5pm | 207 King's Road | www.orlakiely.com/uk | tube Circle, District: Sloane Square*

69B (0) *(R1)*

Organic fashion doesn't sound particularly trendy but this boutique in Hackney is anything but boring. The dresses, jackets, handbags and shoes for women are all designed by labels that work sustainably: Marimekko, Lanius, Beaumont Organic, Komodo. If you come on Sunday you can also visit *Broadway Market*. *Mon–Fri 10:30am–6:30pm, Sat 10am–6pm, Sun noon–6pm | 69B Broadway Market | 69bboutique.com | tube Overground: London Fields*

MARKETS & MARKET STREETS

BOROUGH MARKET ●

(143 F1) *(O6)*

Fruit and vegetables have been sold here since the 13th century. Popular for organic foodstuffs, English farmhouse cheese, delicious pastries, snacks, meat, fresh fish and specialities from all over the globe. If you can, visit on a Thursday, when you won't get trampled in the foodie throng, or Mon/Tue *(10am–5pm)*, when the range of products is slightly limited. *Full market Wed–Fri 10am–5pm, Sat 8am–5pm | corner Borough High St./Stoney St. | www.boroughmarket.org.uk | tube Jubilee, Northern: London Bridge*

BRICK LANE MARKET ★ ●

(136 C3–4) *(Q3–4)*

Street food fans can travel around the globe here: on the street (southwards from Bethnal Green Road) and in the *Boiler House* (no. 152), a hall with food stands. Join the weekend crowd and push past stands with hand-sewn clothes, jewellery, second-hand fashion, vinyl, shoes and all kinds of bric-a-brac – lots and lots of it! At the epicentre lies the *Old Truman Brewery* which houses the *Sunday Up-Market* (only Sun), a paradise for vintage clothing. *Sat 11am–6pm, Sun 10am–5pm | www.bricklanemarket.com | tube Overground: Shoreditch High Street*

BROADWAY MARKET ● (0) *(R1)*

The market with street food, organic fruit and veg is only on Saturdays, but the street between the London Fields park and Regent's Canal is worth a visit on any day: cosy pubs, hip cafés and local designers, e.g. *Fabrications*. Try Violet's Cupcakes with seasonally changing frosting. *Sat 10am–5pm / www.broadwaymarket.co.uk | Overground: London Fields*

CAMDEN MARKET (0) *(⌕ G–H1)*

Colourful, bizarre, extremely popular: this market is for people who love to browse and are not afraid of crowds. Jewellery, clothes, cool design items and food for every taste are for sale. Amy Winehouse fans can take a picture of her statue or visit the pub she used to go to. *Hawley Arms (2 Castlehaven Road). Daily from 10am | www.camdenmarkets.org | tube Northern: Camden Town*

PORTOBELLO ROAD MARKET
(130 B5) (⌕ A5–6)

On Saturdays London's biggest street market for antiques, also glorified junk, fruit and veg: second-hand and designer clothing in the section by the Westway. Best start from the Notting Hill end. *Sat 9am–7pm | Portobello/Golborne Rd. | www.portobelloroad.co.uk | tube Central, Circle, District: Notting Hill Gate*

SPITALFIELDS MARKET
(136 B4) (⌕ P4)

Clothing, jewellery, handbags, greeting cards and much more in a Victorian market hall; on Saturdays INSIDER TIP *Style Market* with trendy designers. *Mon–Fri 10am–5pm, Sun from 9am | 65 Brushfield St. /Commercial St. | www.visitspitalfields.co.uk | tube Liverpool Street*

MUSIC

HMV (132 E5) *(⌕ H5)*

At over 4,600 m² surface area, "His Master's Voice" megastore is the country's largest. *Mon–Sat 8am–9:30pm, Sun noon–6pm | 363 Oxford St. | www.hmv.com | tube Bakerloo, Central, Victoria: Oxford Circus*

ROUGH TRADE EAST ●
(136 C3–4)(⌕ Q4)

Record shop with excellent selection of indie, rock, dance, country, folk and styles that you've never heard of, offering handy listening posts. Regular INSIDER TIP in-store live gigs, mostly at 7pm, frequently free. Well informed shop assistants. *Mon–Thu 9am–9pm, Fri/Sat 10am–8pm, Sun 11am–7pm | Old Truman Brewery |*

TIME TO CHILL

Shopping is tiring, so treat yourself to a relaxing break. The ● *Casa Spa* **(131 E3)** *(⌕ D4) (Wed–Mon 11am–1pm | 439 Edgware Road | tel. 77 24 20 30 | www.casaspa.co.uk | tube Bakerloo: Edgware Road)* on the Arab-influenced Edgware Road in West London offers one of the few authentic hammam experiences in town. Steam bath, robust all-over body peeling with olive-argile clay mud, honey hair mask. Or relax for half a day at the ● *Palm Court Chuan Spa* **(133 D4)** *(⌕ H5) (Tue–Thu from 11am | 1 C Portland Place, Regent St. | from £210 | book ahead at: tel. 76 36 10 00 | palm-court.co.uk/#/afternoon-tea/spa-and-tea | tube Green Park)* with their *Tea Therapy*: salt sauna, massage, tea ritual and then an afternoon tea at the *Palm Court* (see p. 64).

Office has the latest footwear trends

91 Brick Lane | www.roughtrade.com | tube Liverpool Street

SHOES

NIKE RUNNING STORE
(134 A5) (𝄃 K5–6)

There are several Nike stores in London but only in this one are running movements analysed so that runners can find the ultimate running shoes. Once bought, these can be put to the test at the weekly *Run Club*; sign up online! *Mon–Sat 10am–8pm, Sun noon–6pm | 14–15 Neal Street | www.nike.com/gb/en_gb/c/countries/unitedkingdom | tube Piccadilly: Covent Garden*

OFFICE
(134 A5) (𝄃 K5)

From wearable to crazy and not too expensive: ladies and mens' shoes in quirky shapes, patterns and materials, as well as the famous Hunter wellies. *Mon–Sat 10am–8pm, Sun 11am–7pm | 57 Neal St. |*

www.office.co.uk | tube Piccadilly: Covent Garden

PEPONITA & FRIENDS
(136 C1) (𝄃 Q3)

Say goodbye to blisters! A cooperative designs the comfortable high block heels in vintage design in which one can even go on a hike. *Thu 5pm–7pm, Fri/Sat noon–3pm, Sun 9am–5pm, Mon–Wed only by appointment | tel. 0 77 73 08 03 37 | 160 Columbia Road | www.peponita.com | tube Overground: Hoxton*

VIVOBAREFOOT 🌏 (134 A5) (𝄃 K5–6)

The philosophy of these shoes is based on the concept of walking barefoot: next to having minimal fittings, these shoes have an extreme thin sole. They are made of recyclable materials and produced under ethically correct conditions. *Mon–Sat 10:30am–7pm, Sun noon–6pm | 64 Neal St. | www.vivobarefoot.com/uk | tube Piccadilly: Covent Garden*

ENTERTAINMENT

On London's theatre stages you can get to see stars such as Benedict Cumberbatch or Keira Knightly, clubs and young British musicians are creating new trends and the pubs where people meet for drinks after work are like an extension of their living rooms. Top-class symphony orchestras, dance troupes and musical productions are also part of the entertainment business. London's nightlife is many things but never boring!

Traditional *spit and sawdust* pubs are increasingly making way for bars and gastropubs that serve interesting beers and more imaginative food. Standard opening times are Mon–Sat 11am–11pm, Sun noon–10:30pm; the drinking always winds down with the dreaded call for "last orders!" and "time, please!" to finish your drink. Since the reform of the licensing laws, some pubs now have extended opening hours, but usually only at weekends. The club scene, from

Enjoy the unique variety of London's nightlife: traditional pubs, rousing musicals, world-class classical concerts, trendy clubs

super clubs to tiny basement DJ bars, follows fast-moving trends. The hippest club nights for house, techno, hip-hop, R&B, electroclash or dubstep happen at changing venues.

The expensive premiere-screening cinemas boasting the best sound cluster around Leicester Square. Tickets cost about £14–24; matinees and Mondays are cheaper. Try and make time for one of the 150 comedy clubs or a pub evening with stand-up improvisation comedy. Always right on the pulse of the city with tips for going out, including freebies is the listings magazine "Time Out" (print version Tuesdays in central tube stations or see *www.timeout.com/london*). The free "Evening Standard" newspaper *(www.standard.co.uk)* also offers information on musicals, concerts etc. *www.londonnightguide.com* helps you with guest-list booking and table reservation as well as ordering theatre, cinema or concert tickets by credit card using What's App *(tel. 0752 3 528 885)*.

BARS

ABSOLUT ICE BAR
(133 E6) (📖 H6)

Literally a pretty cool place: the temperature at this branch of the Swedish *Ice Bar* is minus 5 degrees Celsius (23°F) all year round. Everything apart from the ceiling is made of ice: walls, tables, decorations, the glasses for the vodka cocktails. *Daily | £13.50–16.50 incl. cocktail (depending on time of day) | 31–33 Heddon St. | tel. 74 78 89 10 | www.icebar london.com | tube Bakerloo, Piccadilly: Piccadilly Circus*

11am | Victoria House | Bloomsbury Place | tel. 70 25 26 76 | www.allstarlanes.co.uk | tube Central, Piccadilly: Holborn

THE BAR WITH NO NAME ⭐
(0) (📖 M1)

Acclaimed cocktail bar in Islington with innovative creations by Tony Conigliaro, a mixer with a background in art and fashion. £10.50 for seriously shaken and stirred house cocktails is not a bad price actually! Booking advised. *Daily from 5pm | 69 Colebrooke Row | tel. 075 40 52 85 93 | www.69colebrookerow.com | tube Northern: Angel*

All Star Lanes: US-style sports bar with a classier touch

ALL STAR LANES ●
(134 A4) (📖 K4)

In this US-flavoured sports bar for boutique bowling, players enjoy toasting their strikes with champagne or mint julep cocktails. There's another branch on Brick Lane in trendy Shoreditch. *Mon–Thu from 3pm, Fri from noon, Sat/Sun from*

CONNAUGHT BAR ⭐
(132 C6) (📖 G6)

Arguably the best hotel bar in town. Why? The art deco interior creates an atmosphere of luxury and elegance. Dress up for the occasion, sink into one of the comfortable sofas and order a Bond-style martini that will be mixed right in front of you on a trolley. *Daily from 4pm | 16 Carlos Place/corner of Mount St. | tel. 73 14 34 19 | www.the-connaught.co.uk | tube Central, Jubilee: Bond Street*

INSIDER TIP FRANK'S CAFÉ ☆
(0) (*Ⅲ 0*)

Open-air bar with ramshackle chic. How about sipping cocktails *(from £6)* on the roof of an abandoned park house in Peckham, the ultimate hip location for a sun downer with a panoramic view over London. Or you can sit at the roughly hewn wooden tables and chill with beer, wine and cider. If it rains, out comes the red awning. *Summer to 1st Oct, Tue–Fri 5pm–11pm, Sat/Sun from 11am | 95a Rye Lane/10th floor of Peckham Multi-Storey Car Park | entrance next to mulitplex cinema | frankscafe.org.uk | tube Overground: Peckham Rye*

HAPPINESS FORGETS
(136 A2) (*Ⅲ P3*)

One of the best bars in hip Shoreditch. The lighting, comfortable seating and vintage furniture create a cosy atmosphere. Staff can advise you on the choice of cocktail or shake up the mix you desire. Try the Tokyo Collins, the Japanese twist on a Tom Collins. Trendy location: pre-booking required! *Daily 5pm–11pm | 8–9 Hoxton Square | tel. 76 13 03 25 | www.happinessforgets.com | tube Northern: Old Street*

MARK'S BAR AT HIX
(133 E6) (*Ⅲ H/J6*)

The cellar of restaurant *Hix Soho* is a veritable treasure trove of alcoholic cocktail ingredients. Exquisite drinks based on historical recipes are shaken and stirred with know-how and passion. Dancing once a month *(Fri from 10pm)*. *Daily from noon | 66–70 Brewer St. | tel.*

72 92 35 18 | www.hixrestaurants.co.uk/restaurant/marks-bars | tube Piccadilly, Bakerloo: Piccadilly Circus

PERMIT ROOM AT DISHOOM KING'S CROSS (0) (*Ⅲ K1–2*)

Postcolonial bar chic in *Dishoom King's Cross*, one of the popular Iranian Mumbai cafés in the reinvigorated area around Granary Square. Inside the cool Victorian industrial building dark wood, green leather seats and dimmed lights create a pleasant atmosphere. Once you've moved to the front of the waiting line, start looking forward to some great gin cocktails. *Daily | 5 Stable Street | tel. 74 20 93 21 | www.dishoom.com/kings-cross | tube Victoria, Northern: King's Cross*

★ **The Bar With No Name**
Small bar with unusual cocktails
→ **p. 84**

★ **Connaught Bar**
Stylish hotel bar serving first-rate cocktails → **p. 84**

★ **Ministry of Sound**
Dance floor in a bus garage: all night through → **p. 86**

★ **English National Opera**
A delight for ears and eyes and a classical repertoire → **p. 89**

★ **Black Friar**
You won't be in a hurry to leave this beautiful arts and crafts pub → **p. 90**

★ **Old Fountain**
Lovely little pub with large beer selection → **p. 90**

MARCO POLO HIGHLIGHTS

CLUBS & CLUB NIGHTS

INSIDER TIP **SKYLOUNGE** ✵

(136 B6) (*𝄞 P6*)

The glass-encased cocktail bar on the top floor of the "DoubleTree Hilton – Tower of London" offers a wonderful view of London's South Bank, the Thames, the Tower Bridge, the new skyscraper "The Shard" and St Paul's Cathedral. Even cooler in summer for chilling on the attached roof terrace. Indoors tables can be reserved. *Mon–Sat 11am–2am, Sun until 1am | 7 Pepys St. | tel. 77 09 10 43 | doubletree3.hilton.com | tube Central, District: Tower Hill*

CLUBS & CLUB NIGHTS

Partygoers have long been waiting for this: finally *The Night Tube* is here! Clubbers can now travel from one dance location to the next, move around the clock on Fri/Sat, on the Victoria, Central, Jubilee, Northern and Piccadilly tube lines. Current club nights are listed on *www.latenightlondon.co.uk* or *www.designmynight.com*.

CLUB AQUARIUM

(136 A1) (*𝄞 O3*)

Dance floor with pool and Jacuzzi. The sounds and parties change depending on the day of the week: Thu top charts, Fri house & techno, Sat Seventies/Eighties disco funk. *Thu 11pm–6am, Fri/Sun until 7am | £15 | 256–260 Old St. | tel. 07796 85 78 08 | www.clubaquarium. co.uk | tube Northern: Old Street*

MINISTRY OF SOUND ★ ●

(143 E3) (*𝄞 N8*)

In this former bus depot clubbers can dance the night away on several dance floors *(10:30pm–6am | from £22)*, e.g. in *The Box* (with surround sound system) or in the *103 Bar*. Fri there's a long night of trance music, *The Gallery,* Sat techno,

house and electro, Tue the low-budget *Milkshake* party for students *(10pm–3am | from £9)*. *103 Gaunt Street | tel. 77 40 86 82 | www.ministryofsound. com | tube Northern, Bakerloo: Elephant & Castle*

INSIDER TIP **SUPA DUPA FLY**

Do you like R&B, hip-hop and garage rock sounds from the Nineties and early 2000s? Then look out online for the location of the next ultimate London party which changes weekly. Emily Rawson, one of the best British DJanes, spins the discs here; occasional live music. Locations in Camden, Dalston, Shoreditch, Bloomsbury. *Fri/Sat 9pm–3am | book online in advance from £5.50 | www.supa dupaflylove.com | www.facebook.com/ supadupaflylove*

VILLAGE UNDERGROUND

(136 B3) (*𝄞 P4*)

When you see the graffiti outside and the discarded underground carriages on the roof, you know you've come to the right place. The club inside a former Victorian warehouse stages special club nights and live concerts with electro, hip-hop and indie music for a mixed audience – from goths to hipsters and fashion girls. *On varying days, from 7:30pm | from £15 | 54 Holywell Lane | tel. 74 22 75 05 | www. villageunderground.co.uk | tube Overground: Shoreditch High Street*

XOYO

(136 A2) (*𝄞 O3*)

Great clubbing location in an old warehouse in Shoreditch with two dance floors. Top DJs regularly play music here for three ongoing months on Saturday nights. *Fri/Sat 9pm–4am | £5–19 | 32–37 Cowper St. | tel. 74 90 11 98 | www.xoyo. co.uk | tube Northern: Old Street*

Shabby chic: concert in trendy Village Underground

COMEDY

THE COMEDY STORE
(133 F6) (*ØJ6*)

Still the city's most popular comedy club and the place where the alternative comedy scene formed in the Seventies. *Daily from 6:30pm | £14–26 | 1A Oxendon St. | tel. 0844 8 71 76 99 (*) | www.thecomedy store.co.uk | tube Bakerloo, Piccadilly: Piccadilly Circus*

CINEMAS

BFI LONDON IMAX CINEMA
(142 C2) (*Ø L7*)

Experience 3D movies, opera screenings and *all-nighters* on the country's largest screen (26 m/85 ft). *£19–22 | 1 Charlie Chaplin Walk | South Bank | tel. 79 28 32 32 | www.bfi.org.uk/bfi-imax | tube Waterloo*

BRITISH FILM INSTITUTE
(142 C1) (*Ø L7*)

Classic and contemporary movies plus directors' specials: the *British Film Institute* is a paradise for film buffs. About 2,000 films are shown here every year including a lot of brand new ones during the London Film Festival in October. Watch films for free at the ● Mediathèque *(Tue–Sat noon–8pm, Sun 12:30pm–8pm). Daily. 9:45am–11pm / South Bank | tel. 79 28 32 32 | www.bfi.org.uk | tube Waterloo)*

CONCERTS & GIGS

BARBICAN (135 E–F4) (*Ø N–O4*)
Even the locals sometimes get lost in this maze-like residential and cultural complex. The home of the London Symphony Orchestra puts on a truly excellent programme of concerts, exhibi-

tions and theatre. *£10–65 | Silk St. | tel. 76 38 88 91 | www.barbican.org.uk | tube Circle, Hammersmith & City, Metropolitan: Barbican*

CADOGAN HALL (140 B–C4) *(* *F9)*
The concert hall is housed in a tower-topped church formerly used by the Boston Church of Christ sect. Various musical styles, high quality. *5 Sloane Terrace | tel. 77 30 45 00 | www.cadoganhall.com | tube Circle, District: Sloane Square*

RONNIE SCOTT'S (133 F5) *(* *J5)*
Legendary jazz club in Soho where greats such as Miles Davis or Count Basie have played. *Mon–Sat 6pm–3am, Sun 6pm–midnight, Sun jazz lunch noon–4pm | 47 Frith St. | tel. 74 39 07 47 | www.ronnie scotts.co.uk | tube Northern, Piccadilly: Leicester Square*

LOW BUDGET

Current, classics and cult (from £8.50) are on show at the *Prince Charles Cinema* **(133 F6)** *(* *J6).* *(Chinatown | 7 Leicester Place | tel. 74 94 36 54 | www.princecharlescine ma.com | tube Northern, Piccadilly: Leicester Square*

Pick up half-price theatre tickets for the same evening (plus a £3 fee) at the two tkts theatre booths *(www. tkts.co.uk). Tkts Leicester Square* **(133 F6)** *(* *J6) (southern side | Mon–Sat 9am–7pm, Sun 11am–4:30pm | tube Northern, Piccadilly: Leicester Square).* There are two separate windows: one for matinee tickets, the other for evening shows (limited to two tickets per person).

VORTEX JAZZ CLUB (0) *(* *0)*
A popular modern jazz venue for almost 30 years. Well-known jazz stars helped the club win the 2013 live jazz prize and it opens its stage up to young talent (daily 8pm–midnight). They also have a second stage in the downstairs bar where the cocktails have musically fitting names *(Wed/Thu/Sun 6pm–11pm, Fri/Sat 6pm–2am). From £10 | 11 Gillett Square | tel. 72 54 40 97 | www.vortexjazz. co.uk | Dalston Kingsland (Overground)*

CHARLIE AND THE CHOCOLATE FACTORY (134 B6) *(* *K6)*
Academy Award winner Sam Mendes directs this musical based on the classic children's book from Roald Dahl about Charlie Bucket, the recluse chocolate factory owner Willy Wonka and five golden tickets. There are also two film adaptations of the story. *Mon–Sat 7:30, Wed, Sat 2:30pm | £25–70 | Theatre Royal Drury Lane | tel. 0844 8 58 88 77 (*) | www.charlieandthechocolatefactory. com | tube Piccadilly: Covent Garden*

MAMMA MIA! (134 B6) *(* *K6)*
Best of Abba: the hits of the legendary Swedish pop quartett, held together by a thin plot and a high feel-good factor. *£15–68 | Novello Theatre | Aldwych | tel. 0844 4 82 51 15 (*) | www.mamma-mia. com | tube Circle, District: Temple*

MUSIC BARS

CAFÉ OTO (0) *(* *0)*
Oto is Japanese for "sound"; come to listen to up-to-the-minute eclectic sounds in trendily down-at-heel Dalston – accompanied by Persian-inspired snacks, cake and good coffee. *Daily; café closed for soundcheck 5:30pm–7pm | 18–22 Ashwin*

St. | www.cafeoto.co.uk | train: Dalston Kingsland, Dalston Junction (overground)

STAR OF BETHNAL GREEN
(137 D2) (*M R3*)

The hip East End set meets at this cool pub for DJ sets, gigs, comedy shows, quiz and karaoke evenings, roast dinners, games exchanges and other events. Wide choice

Lane | tel. 78 45 93 00 | www.eno.org | tube Northern, Piccadilly: Leicester Square

INSIDER TIP ▶ KING'S HEAD
(0) (*M M1*)

Classically trained singers keep 100 guests entertained with modern versions of classical operas. The atmosphere in London's

Swords at the ready at the English National Opera

of affordable dishes. *359 Bethnal Green | tel. 74 58 44 80 | www.starofbethnal green.com | tube Central: Bethnal Green*

OPERA

ENGLISH NATIONAL OPERA ★
(134 A6) (*M K6*)

The ENO at the Coliseum is home to classical opera repertoire sung in English. How does the *Secret Seats* lottery work? Buy a ticket online for £20 and you'll be guaranteed a seat worth £30 or more on the night. *Tickets £12–125 | St Martin's*

oldest pub theatre (since 1970) is cosy and familiar and for only £15 you get to sit right in the middle of the action, possible participation included (book in advance, only people on the guest list are allowed in). *115 Upper St. | www.kingsheadtheatre. com | tube Northern: Angel*

ROYAL ALBERT HALL
(139 E3) (*M D8*)

London musical institution with a large selection of concerts. Recommended: the *Proms* concerts in summer *(£8–68 | tel. 75 89 82 12).* See p. 32.

ROYAL OPERA HOUSE
(134 A5) (*𝄞 K5–6*)

World-famous opera house and ballet. The beautifully restored *Paul Hamlyn Hall* is open to the public *(Mon–Fri 10am–3:30pm)*. INSIDER TIP Stand-by tickets at half price are sold four hours before performance; each Friday at 1pm 49 tickets for the following week are sold. Take the backstage tour (call to book a space) to take a peek behind the scenes. *£8–250 | Bow St. | tel. 73 04 40 00 | www. roh.org.uk | tube Piccadilly: Covent Garden*

PUBS

BLACK FRIAR ★ ●
(135 D6) (*𝄞 M6*)

London's most beautiful arts-and-crafts-style pub is stunning. Watching out above the entrance is the statue of a monk; inside a mixed crowd drink between bronze reliefs and marble. Unsure which ale to go for? "Sip before you sup" grants you a free taster. Including authentic pub food, for example *sausage and mash. 174 Queen Victoria St. | tel. 72 36 54 74 | tube Circle, District: Blackfriars*

BULL AND LAST
(0) (*𝄞 0*)

Handy for solid sustenance after a stroll on Hampstead Heath: cosy pub, upstairs family-friendly restaurant. *168 Highgate Road | tel. 72 67 36 41 | www.thebulland last.co.uk | tube Northern: Kentish Town*

THE DOVE ● (0) (*𝄞 0*)

This wonderfully atmospheric riverside pub is 400 years old! ⚲ The conservatory is an ideal vantage point, not only for the Oxford-Cambridge boats race in March. *19 Upper Mall | tel. 87 48 94 74 | www.dovehammersmith.co.uk | tube District: Ravenscourt Park*

OLD FOUNTAIN ★
(135 F2) (*𝄞 O3*)

Cosy pub with garden terrace and a huge beer selection: real ales, craft beer, bottled beer. You'll need to do some ser-

Traditional pub with opulent decor: Black Friar

ious drinking to try them all. Probably better to come back again! *3 Baldwin Street | tel. 72 53 29 70 | twitter.com/ oldfountainales | tube Northern: Old Street*

RED LION (141 E1) *(📖 J6)*

The ambience in this Victorian gin palace in chic St James is friendly. *Mon–Sat from 11:30am | 2 Duke of York St. | tel. 73 21 07 82 | www.redlionmayfair.co.uk | tube Circle, District: Piccadilly Circus, St James's Park*

THE SALISBURY (134 A6) *(📖 K6)*

One of the prettiest Victorian gin palaces in town – mahogany wood and engraved glass everywhere. Central location for the West End theatres. *90 St Martin's Lane | tel. 78 36 58 63 | tube Northern, Piccadilly: Leicester Square*

THEATRE & DANCE

DONMAR WAREHOUSE
(134 A5) *(📖 K5)*

Rising star of the London theatre scene, with the occasional Hollywood star on the stage. *41 Earlham St. | tel. 0844 8 71 76 24 (*) | www.donmarwarhouse.com | tube Northern, Piccadilly: Leicester Square*

NATIONAL THEATRE
(142 C1) *(📖 L6–7)*

Britain's renowned national theatre unites three stages *(Cottesloe, Lyttleton, Olivier)*, staging classical and contemporary plays. *Tickets from £15 | South Bank | tel. 74 52 30 00 | www.nationaltheatre.org.uk | tube Waterloo*

SADLER'S WELLS THEATRE
(135 D2) *(📖 M2–3)*

Experience the best British and international troupes in action at the country's leading dance venue. *Form £31 | Rosebery*

Av. | tel. 78 63 80 00 | www.sadlerswells. com | tube Northern: Angel

SOHO THEATRE
(133 F5) *(📖 J5)*

A success story on the London theatre circuit, with a good mix of new English and international plays and comedy. *From £12.50 | 21 Dean St. | tel. 74 78 01 00 | www.sohotheatre.com | tube Central, Northern: Tottenham Court Road*

WINE BARS

PEPITO (134 A–B1) *(📖 K2)*

Delicious tapas! Small Andalusian sherry bar with cosy *bodega* ambience in London. *Mon–Fri 5pm–midnight, Sat from 6pm | 3 Varnishers Yard | tel. 78 41 73 31 | www.camino.co.uk/barpepito | tube King's Cross*

TERROIRS (134 A6) *(📖 K6)*

Unusual wines made by small producers. The cheese selection is as French as the friendly waiters. *Mon–Sat noon–11pm | 5 William IV St. | tel. 70 36 06 60 | www. terroirswinebar.com | tube Bakerloo, Northern: Charing Cross*

24-HOUR LONDON

BRICK LANE BEIGEL BAKE
(136 C3) *(📖 Q3)*

This bakery is an institution. Cheap bagels with salmon, cream cheese, salted beef. Standing only. *Daily 24 hours | 159 Brick Lane | tube Overground: Shoreditch*

TINSELTOWN (135 D4) *(📖 M4)*

While London is asleep, check your mails in this American diner over a milkshake. *Mon–Sat noon–4am, Sun until 3am | 44– 46 St John St. | tel. 76 89 24 24 | www.tinsel town.co.uk | tube Circle, Hammersmith & City, Metropolitan: Farringdon*

WHERE TO STAY

There are many different kinds of places you can lay your head in London, from expensive hotels to cheap hostels, from designer apartments to houseboats. The range of prices is, as with most other things, above the UK average. Look out for early bird and online discounts or cheaper weekend rates.

When you book, check if the price includes breakfast and VAT (20 per cent) – which is often not the case with higher category hotels. If you book online, also check in which currency (British pounds or other) the price is quoted. And it's always a good idea to enquire about special rates.

Solo travellers are penalised, as *single occupancy* costs about two thirds of the double-room rate. Small groups or families often have the choice of a room with several beds.

Apart from the low-price sector, rooms are normally *en-suite* with private bathroom. Bed & breakfast is practically a British invention. Usually you have to pay cash; prices are inclusive of VAT. In the mid-price sector the boundary between hotels and B & B can be fluid. Thankfully, both are gradually moving away from chintzy curtains and flowery embroidery. Instead of the full English breakfast with eggs, sausages and bacon, there's increasingly a continental breakfast on offer, with cereals, yoghurt, toast and jam.

Bookings usually have to be secured with a credit card. On *www.visitlondonoffers. com (tel. 01904 71 73 84 [*])* you can find

Photo: 40 Winks Hotel

First things first: where do we lay our heads? Here is a small selection of recommended hotels, B & Bs, apartments and hostels

hotels in all categories as well as packages including opera or theatre tickets. *Premier Inn* is a cheap British hotel chain with comfortable beds (from £70 for a double room).

More and more B & Bs now also offer their residents a good-value dinner. For a private room in a Londoner's home, try the *At Home in London agency (tel. 87 48 27 01 | www.athomeinlondon.co. uk)* which you can browse by central location or tube station. *www.londonbb.com* has B & Bs and apartments on offer.

Visitors staying a week or longer can book a whole flat on *www.holidaylettings. co.uk*. *www.budgetplaces.com* is the address for low-budget accommodation in the city.

APARTMENTS

CASTLETOWN HOUSE
(138 A6) (*Ø* A10)
Family-run house in West London with five apartments of varying sizes ranging from a studio for two to a three-bed flat

Living on Bermondsey Square – modern, friendly, trendy

for 6 persons; all rooms with bathroom, kitchen, Wi-Fi, TV and some with own washing machine. *11 Castletown Road | tel. 73 86 94 23 | www.castletownhouse. co.uk | tube District, Piccadilly: West Kensington, Barons Court |* Moderate

23 GREENGARDEN HOUSE
(132 C5) (*⑪ G5*)
Well-equipped, bright and friendly apartments (modern country-house style) on car-free St Christopher's Place, a few yards from Oxford Street. *23 aps. | £260–460 | St Christopher's Place | tel. 79 35 91 91 | www.greengardenhouse.com | tube Central, Jubilee: Bond Street |* Expensive

INSIDER TIP ▶ B & B BELGRAVIA
(141 D4) (*⑪ G9*)
Pleasant B & B in chic Belgravia. 17 rooms have been stylishly refurbished with a contemporary decor, rooms available from £140; ◐ organic breakfast in the morning; excellent location. For those planning a longer break in the city, the B & B offers 9 studios with kitchen from £110 *(82 Ebury St). 64–66 Ebury St. | tel. 72 59 85 70 | www.bb-belgravia.com | tube Circle, District: Victoria*

THE COACHHOUSE (0) (*⑪ 0*)
The motto is: "Live like a local". Country charm, half an hour from the city centre. If the pretty coach-house cottage is fully booked – it is very popular – former army officer Harley and his wife Meena can arrange private apartments through their trusted network. *1 ap. | 2 Tunley Road | tel. 87 72 19 39 | www.coachhouse.chslondon. com | tube Northern: Balham*

HAMPSTEAD VILLAGE GUESTHOUSE
(0) (*⑪ 0*)
Friendly B & B in green Hampstead, only 20 minutes from the centre. Flexible

breakfast, from 8am (Sat/Sun 9am) till late in the morning, in summer in the garden. *9 rooms | (en-suite double £180) 1 garden flat with kitchen (sleeping 5: £200 without breakfast), 2 Kemplay Road | tel. 74 35 86 79 | www.humpsteadguesthouse.com | tube Northern: Hampstead*

MARBLE ARCH INN
(140 B5) *(ØD F5)*

Centrally located B & B (close to Hyde Park and Oxford Street); 29 small, plainly decorated rooms. Family room (for up to 6 people) available; double rooms from £105 (without breakfast). *49–50 Upper Berkeley St. | tel. 77 23 78 88 | www.marblearch-inn.co.uk | tube Central: Marble Arch*

113 PEPYS ROAD (0) *(ØD 0)*

East meets West in South London. The bamboo blinds, kimonos and Chinese porcelain of the three rooms reflect the travels of the English-Chinese owner. Besides a traditional full English breakfast Chinese noodle soup is also served on request. Personal touch, nice garden. Double room £130. *New Cross Gate | tel. 76 39 10 60 | www.pepysroad.com | tube Overground: New Cross Gate*

HOTELS: EXPENSIVE

BERMONDSEY SQUARE
(144 B3) *(ØD P8)*

Super-friendly and in a hip location on Bermondsey Square. A suite on the top floor features hammocks, the Lucy Suite boasts a ✂ **INSIDERTIP** hot tub on the roof terrace – for a whirlpool session with VIP view! Great location to explore the Thames South Bank: Tate Modern, The Shard, Shakespeare's Globe, Borough Market all within reach. Shop in the cool Bermondsey Street, have brunch in *Village East* at the weekend or sip gin

and cocktails at *214 Bermondsey. 90 rooms | Tower Bridge Road | tel. 73 78 24 50 | www.bermondseysquarehotel. co.uk | tube London Bridge*

DOUBLETREE BY HILTON HOTEL LONDON – WESTMINSTER
(142 A4) *(ØD K9)*

Award-winning hotel near the *Tate Britain.* Contemporary design, friendly service, love for details, good restaurant. *460 rooms | 30 John Islip St. | tel. 76 30 10 00 | doubletree3.hilton.com | tube Victoria: Pimlico*

HAZLITT'S ★
(133 F5) *(ØD J5)*

Wonderfully old-fashioned literary hotel in the heart of Soho. Essayist and critic William Hazlitt (1778–1830) lived and died here, allegedly of exorbitantly high tea consumption. *23 rooms | 6 Frith*

★ **Hazlitt's**
Old-fashioned charm with literary connections → p. 95

★ **Church Street Hotel**
Trendy yet unpretentious in Camberwell → p. 98

★ **The Fielding Hotel**
You can't get more central → p. 97

★ **The Z Hotel Shoreditch**
Small rooms, central location → p. 99

★ **The Savoy**
A legend with eco touch → p. 96

★ **The Ritz**
Tradition, luxury in style → p. 96

MARCO POLO HIGHLIGHTS

Hazlitt's Hotel in Soho scores with stylish rooms

Street | Soho Square | tel. 74 34 17 71 | www.hazlittshotel.com | tube Central, Northern: Tottenham Court Road

ONE ALDWYCH HOTEL 🌐
(134 B5–6) *(Ⓜ K–L6)*

5-star accommodation with green comfort: a chlorine-free swimming pool with underwater music, organic care and beauty products. Family rooms and baby-sitting service. *105 rooms and suites | 1 Aldwych | tel. 73 00 10 00 | www.onealdwych.com | tube Piccadilly: Covent Garden*

THE RITZ ⭐ (141 E1) *(Ⓜ H7)*

Probably London's most famous hotel, with views of Green Park. Rooms are opulently furnished with antique Louis XVI furniture, in combinations of the classic Ritz colour palette of blue, peach, pink and yellow. Personal service is not just a word here: when guests are still "Madam" or "Sir", it somehow sounds right. *136 rooms | 150 Piccadilly | tel. 74 93 81 81 | www.theritzlondon.com | tube Jubilee, Piccadilly, Victoria: Green Park*

THE SAVOY ⭐ 🌐 (134 B6) *(Ⓜ K6)*

125-year-old traditional establishment with celebrated guests such as Winston Churchill, Frank Sinatra and Katharine Hepburn. Its refurbishment has returned the hotel to its former glory. The hotel is now eco-friendly: recycling of the kitchen's heat, hotel transfer by hybrid car, organic produce and eco-tours through London. *267 rooms | Strand | tel. 78 36 43 43 | www.fairmont.com/savoy-london | tube Charing Cross*

TAJ 51 BUCKINGHAM GATE
(141 E3) *(Ⓜ H–J8)*

Yes! A child-friendly luxury hotel! 82 suites and apartments, all with kitchen. The mini bathrobes, a cup of hot chocolate in the evening and a child-friendly menu in the restaurant will keep kids happy. *51 Buckingham Gate | tel. 77 69 77 66 |*

www.taj51buckinghamgate.co.uk | tube Victoria

W HOTEL (137 F6) (*ш J6*)

Five-star fashion hotel on Leicester Square with disco balls, huge screens, iPod docks, vibrators in the minibar and vinyl record room service. *192 rooms | 10 Wardour Street | tel. 7758 10 00 | www.wlondon.co.uk | tube Northern, Piccadilly: Leicester Square*

HOTELS: MODERATE

THE FIELDING HOTEL ★
(134 B5) (*ш K5*)

Super-central for the West End, yet in a quiet courtyard location opposite the Royal Opera House; very popular with the acting crowd. No breakfast, instead plenty of lovely cafés outside the front door.
● INSIDER TIP Free access to the spa next door! *24 rooms | 4 Broad Court | tel. 78 36 83 05 | www.thefieldinghotel.co.uk | tube Piccadilly: Covent Garden*

HOXTON HOTEL (136 A2) (*ш O–P3*)

A good location in Shoreditch, contemporary design and a light breakfast distinguish this hotel with 210 rooms. ● Recycling and energy efficiency are high on the hotel's agenda. Clubbers don't have far to go to fall into bed, and rates go down from Friday to Sunday. Have your name put on the mailing list and hunt the best-value online offers. *81 Great Eastern St. | tel. 75 50 10 00 | www.hoxtonhotels.com | tube Northern: Old Street*

THE NADLER KENSINGTON ●
(139 D5) (*ш C9–10*)

Located in the vicinity of several museums in Kensington, this hotel has small but affordable rooms with mini kitchens. Breakfast (if booked) is brought to your room in a take-away bag. Ecological touch: energy-saving lights and water-saving toilet flush. *65 rooms | 25 Courtfield Gardens | tel. 72 44 22 55 | www.nadlerhotels. com/the-nadler-kensington.html | tube District: Earl's Court*

RAFAYEL ON THE LEFT BANK ●
(0) (*ш 0*)

In case you want to appease your ecological conscience: this boutique hotel by the river uses LED lights, rainwater, recycled glass and paper and organic care products. For a view of the river book one of the larger ➤ rooms with glass walls. *65 rooms | 34 Lombard Road | tel. 78 01 36 10 | www.hotelrafayel.com | tube Overground: Clapham Junction*

STYLOTEL (135 F5) (*ш D5*)

The design of the 40 rooms and 8 suites with kitchenette is trendy and futuristic: lots of metal and a minimalist colour

LOW BUDGET

In the summer college break, *Imperial College London* (139 F3) (*ш D8*) (*Watts Way | Princes Gardens | tel. 75 94 97 12 | www.3imperial.ac.uk/summeraccommodation | tube Circle, District, Piccadilly: South Kensington*) offers 722 large, centrally located rooms, incl. breakfast and access to gym and swimming pool from £81.

Interesting for Heathrow and Gatwick travellers: at the new Japanese-inspired *Yotel* (0) (*ш 0*) pod hotel (*tel. 71 00 11 00 | www.yotel.com*), the designer standard cabin costs £62 (depending on the airport), the premium version £85. Also bookable for just four hours (£56/£69)!

scheme. Located close to tube and bus stations. English breakfast on request. *160–162 Sussex Gardens | tel. 020 77 23 10 26 | www.stylotel.com | tube Bakerloo, Circle: Paddington*

40 WINKS (137 F3) *(⊞ S4)*

Get your 40 winks in this unique place. The two rooms share a bathroom, but the hip factor compensates. This stylish celebrity favourite in the cool East End is suited to travellers who love staying in a magazine shoot. Book well in advance! *2 rooms | 109 Mile End Road | tel. 77 90 02 59 | www.40winks.org | tube Stepney Green*

HOTELS: BUDGET

ALHAMBRA HOTEL (134 A2) *(⊞ K3)*

If you're travelling by Eurostar, this family-run residence is just a few metres away from St Pancras Station. Close to

MORE THAN A GOOD NIGHT'S SLEEP

London lullaby

Not so far out as it seems: the DLR runs to the old docklands in the east where this floating dream in white is anchored. From the luxury cabins of the hotel yacht *Sunborn London* **(0)** *(⊞ 0) (131 rooms and 4 suites | Royal Victoria Dock | tel. 37 14 81 11 | www.sunborn hotels.com/london | tube DLR: Custom House | Expensive)* you can see the skyline of Canary Wharf, the O_2 Arena and the docks. The gentle motion of the water will rock you to sleep like a baby.

Splashes of colour

A happy Mexican symphony in colour in south London with a broad range of individually decorated rooms, with colourfully tiled bathrooms and L'Occitane toiletries. The spacious community bar in the ★ *Church Street Hotel* **(0)** *(⊞ 0) (31 rooms | 29–33 Camberwell Church Street | tel. 77 03 59 84 | www.churchstreethotel.com | various buses | Moderate)* with coffee, tea and drinks runs as an honesty bar. Nowhere near a tube, but with a cool art café across the street *(www.dailygoods london.com)* and the *Camberwell Market,* a street food market (Sun), around the corner.

Square but fair

Original minimalistic design ideas: a ladder turns into a shelf, the lamp shade is made out of a garden hose and the room itself is cubic. A giant poster above the bed, a tv at the foot of the bed and a bathroom that is connected with the bed post add to the overall funky flair anc cubic chic of the *Qbic Hotel* **(136 C5)** *(⊞ Q5) (171 room | 42 Adler Street | tel. 020 30 21 33 00 | qbichotels.com/de/ london-city | tube Hammersmith & City, District: Aldgate East | Budget).* You can rent a bike and if you only want to sleep here, why not book one of the cheap rooms without windows?

Arresting

For guests who like their accomodation cosy and cheap: The stylish *Clink78 Hostel* **(134 B2)** *(⊞ L3) (100 rooms | 78 King's Cross Road | tel. 71 83 94 00 | www.clinkhostel.com | tube King's Cross | Budget)* in a former courthouse lets you sleep "behind bars" in Japanese-inspired pods.

the British Library and British Museum. *52 rooms, cheaper without bathroom | 17–19 Argyle St .| tel. 78 37 95 75 | www. alhambrahotel.com | tube Northern, Piccadilly, Victoria, Circle: King's Cross*

RIDGEMOUNT HOTEL
(133 F3–4) (*∅ J4*)

Traditional Bloomsbury family-run affair with a lot of repeat business. Not all of the smallish rooms have their own bathroom (room sleeping five £170). Garden. *32 rooms | 65–67 Gower St. | tel. 76 36 11 41 | www.ridgemounthotel.co.uk | tube Northern: Goodge Street*

RUSHMORE HOTEL
(138 C5) (*∅ B9*)

22 individually furnished rooms with murals. A good breakfast buffet spread is laid out in the conservatory. *11 Trebovir Road | tel. 73 70 38 39 | www.rushmore-hotel.co.uk | tube District, Piccadilly: Earl's Court*

THE Z HOTEL SHOREDITCH ★
(135 F2) (*∅ O3*)

Price and trendy location are the outstanding features of this hotel in a former administration building; the stylish rooms are equipped with large TV screens, breakfast buffet can be booked separately. *111 rooms | 136–144 City Road | tel. 35 51 37 02 | www.thezhotels.com/z-shoreditch | tube Northern: Old Street*

Cubic chic: Qbic

HOSTELS, CAMPING & MORE

BUSH HOUSEBOAT
(0) (*∅ O*)

Original self-catering option: a houseboat in west London, quarter of an hour to the city centre. Sundowners on deck, dinners in the steering cabin. *School holidays only | www.bushhouseboat.co.uk | tube District, Overground: Kew Gardens*

KEYSTONE HOUSE (134 B1) (*∅ K2*)

Welcoming King's Cross hostel with just under 160 beds (from £29, breakfast next door: £3.50) and personal atmosphere. Separate women's dorm. 24-hour reception. *272–276 Pentonville Road | tel. 78 37 64 44 | www.keystone-house.com | tube King's Cross, St Pancras*

LEE VALLEY CAMPING & CARAVAN PARK (0) (*∅ O*)

Glamping in action: campsite with heated cabins with two army beds each and electric light for £35 and pitches for backpackers with their own tent (£15–23). Travelling time to the city centre: one hour. *Meridian Way | tel. 88 03 69 00 | www.visitleevalley. org.uk | tube Victoria: Tottenham Hale, then train to Ponders End*

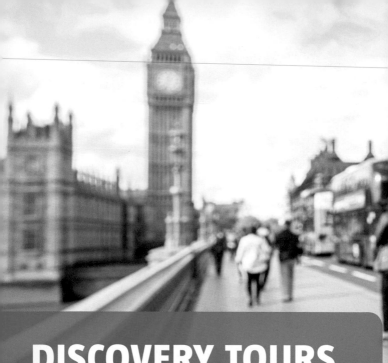

DISCOVERY TOURS

① LONDON AT A GLANCE

START: ① Simpson's-in-the-Strand **END:** ⑫ Chandos		**1 day** Walking time (without stops) 2 ¾ hours
Distance: ➡ 9.8 km/6 miles		

COSTS: one-day bus and tube ticket £12.10, admissions £75, food and drink £110

WHAT TO PACK: camera, jacket and tie for the Ritz!

IMPORTANT TIPS: remember to book in advance for the ⑪ **English National Opera** as well as for afternoon tea at ⑩ **The Ritz**. Gentlemen are required to wear a jacket and tie for the Ritz.
During the week the last tube departs at midnight. Changing of the guards takes place every day at 11am (Sun 10am) at the ③ **Horse Guards Building**.

Would you like to explore the places that are unique to this city? Then the Discovery Tours are just the thing for you – they include terrific tips for stops worth making, breathtaking places to visit, selected restaurants and fun activities. It's even easier with the Touring App: download the tour with map and route to your smartphone using the QR Code on pages 2/3 or from the website address in the footer below – and you'll never get lost again even when you're offline.

TOURING APP

→ p. 2/3

This one-day tour takes you right through the centre of London to discover the best sights and most noteworthy attractions: it starts in the centre with its wide choice of outstanding museums and then onto Parliament, Westminster Abbey and ends with a cultural performance in the evening. Get acquainted with the city's landmarks on this relaxed one-day tour.

08:00am Start your first day in London with a great British fry-up of sausages, eggs and bacon in the traditional establishment ❶ **Simpson's-in-the-Strand** → p. 68 situated right next door to the famous Savoy Hotel. After this

❶ Simpson's-in-the-Strand 🍽

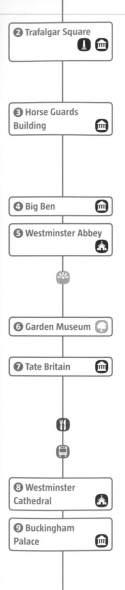

❷ Trafalgar Square

❸ Horse Guards Building

❹ Big Ben

❺ Westminster Abbey

❻ Garden Museum

❼ Tate Britain

❽ Westminster Cathedral

❾ Buckingham Palace

hearty breakfast, walk **in a westerly direction along The Strand** to ❷ **Trafalgar Square** → p. 44, the geographical centre of the city with the towering landmark of **Nelson's Column**. Take time out of your busy schedule to visit the **National Gallery** → p. 43. Then head **down Whitehall** to the corridors of power.

11:00am Time your tour so that you arrive at the ❸ **Horse Guards Building** → p. 36 at 11am (Sun 10am) for the daily changing of the guard. However the bearskin-topped cavalry soldiers are there all day, stoically serving as a photo opportunity for thousands of snapshots; the most daring tourists even pat their horses! Then it's **past Downing Street No. 10 and along Whitehall** to ❹ **Big Ben** → p. 36, the clock tower of the **Houses of Parliament** → p. 36, the "mother" of all parliaments, and to ❺ **Westminster Abbey** → p. 38. **After crossing Westminster Bridge, the inspiration for William Wordsworth's famous sonnet in 1802, take a walk along the southern bank of the Thames from where you have amazing views of the imposing golden ensemble of the Houses of Parliament on the opposite bank. Take a closer look at the gardens belonging to the** ❻ **Garden Museum** → p. 54, before **crossing Lambeth Bridge.**

01:00pm Along **Millbank** you'll reach ❼ **Tate Britain** → p. 37, the temple of British art. Take time to enjoy a fascinating trip through 500 years of British art: from William Blake, William Turner to Henry Moore and Lucian Freud. As part of your tour, enjoy lunch in the traditional and picturesque restaurant **Rex Whistler** *(tel. 78 87 88 25 | www.tate.org.uk | Moderate)*. Then continue from here **by bus (nos. 2, 36, 185, 436 from Vauxhall Bridge Road) to Victoria Station. To the right, on Victoria Street,** you'll see the unusual ❽ **Westminster Cathedral** → p. 39 set slightly back from the road. With its red-and-white banded façade, this cathedral is only 100 years old. A stroll **along Palace Street** brings you to ❾ **Buckingham Palace** → p. 34, the Queen's city residence. In August and September, when the lady of the house is away at Balmoral, you can view selected rooms of the palace.

05:00pm Take a brief look down the The Mall, the city's landmark ceremonial approach road to the palace and Admiralty Arch, before you **continue in the direction of**

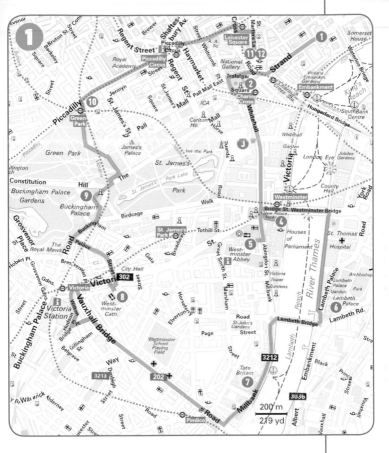

Green Park and tube station with the same name for a perfect afternoon tea with sandwiches and scones at the legendary ⑩ **The Ritz → p. 64**. Remember to book well in advance and wear the obligatory jacket and tie. Have you forgotten yours? Then don't worry, simply head to Fortnum & Mason → p. 76 and enjoy your afternoon tea there.

06:30pm Work off the cake by walking to **Piccadilly Circus → p. 44**, and then via Coventry and Cranbourn Street to tube station Leicester Square. Turn right into Charing Cross Road: after about 15 min. you will reach the ⑪ **English National Opera → p. 89**. After the show (book in ad-

⑩ The Ritz

⑪ English National Opera

⓬ Chandos

vance!) why not have a last drink in the pub ⓬ **Chandos**
(daily 11am–11pm | 29 St Martin's Lane | tel. 78 36 14 01).

2

THROUGH THE EAST END: CURRY, VINTAGE AND GRAFFITI

START: ❶ Liverpool Street Station END: ⓭ Old Street	½ day Walking time (without stops) 1½ hours
Distance: ➡ 4.5 km/2.8 miles	
COSTS: admissions £20, food and drink £40	
IMPORTANT TIPS: ❷ **Dennis Severs House.** During the day only open Sun and Mon; if you want to visit in the evening (Mon, Wed, Fri), reserve in advance! The last tube on weekdays runs at midnight.	

The fringes of the City with its glitzy office towers merge with the old East End where in Victorian times the prostitute killer Jack the Ripper roamed. Hip bars and clubs have taken root here as well as a creative designer and street artist scene.

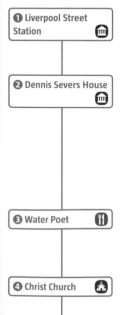

❶ Liverpool Street Station 🏛

❷ Dennis Severs House 🏛

❸ Water Poet 🍽

❹ Christ Church 🏰

12:00pm Start at ❶ **Liverpool Street Station**, a busy light-filled cathedral of the golden railway age, cast-iron roof girders and palmiform columns. **Take the Bishopsgate exit and take a left along Bishopsgate, lined by post-modern office architecture. Turn right into Folgate Street** and visit ❷ **Dennis Severs House** *(Sun noon–4pm, Mon noon–2pm, 5pm–9pm, Wed, Fri 5pm–9pm | during the day £10 (book ahead) £15 in the evening | 18 Folgate St. | tel. 72 47 40 13 | www.dennissevershouse.co.uk)*, a 300-year-old residence belonging to a Huguenot silk weaving family. This is a special experience: the tour takes you on a trip into the past which makes you believe you have met the weaving family even though you haven't actually seen them but have heard and smelt them with their half-eaten food and lit candles on table and the fire still burning in the fireplace. The ❸ **Water Poet** pub *(daily noon–1pm | tel. 74 26 04 95 | www.waterpoet.co.uk | Budget)* across the street is a good spot for a quick break. **Then turn right again into busy Commercial Street.** Opposite the friendly shops, pubs and cafés around **Spitalfields Market → p. 80 at the crossroads with Fournier Street** is ❹ **Christ Church** *(Mon–Fri 10am–4pm, Sun 1pm–4pm | ccspitalfields.org)* from 1729, a masterpiece by Nicholas Hawksmoor. Christopher Wren's gifted pupil was a mysterious personality with a penchant for pagan symbolism, pyramids and obelisks. **Cross Fournier Street** to reach the famous ❺ **Brick Lane**. In the 18th century, Huguenot silk weavers lived here; it was then home to a sizable Jewish community and later Bengali textile workers. Thus evolved "Banglatown" with sari shops, Bengali sweet shops and curry restaurants; these days the restaurants prevail and a few new independent stores and street food places have popped up. House no. 59, on the **corner of Fournier Street/Brick Lane,** is one of the most symbolic buildings of the East End: formerly a Huguenot church, later a Methodist chapel, then a synagogue and now since the mid-1970s the **Brick Lane Mosque.** INSIDERTIP▸ Graffiti and street art can be seen on the right in ❻ **Princelet Street** and on the right in ❼ **Hanbury Street**. Keep your eyes peeled as besides the striking paintings, if you look hard enough, you'll also see smaller wall installations which are often painted over and refreshed regularly. Maybe you'll even spot a Banksy original.

03:00pm How about a break? **Back on Brick Lane** try a curry or a Balti dish from the Kashmir region in ❽ **Aladin** (Mon–Thu noon–midnight, Fri/Sat noon–1am, Sun

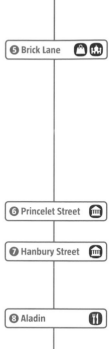

❺ Brick Lane 🛍️ 🏛️

❻ Princelet Street 🏛️

❼ Hanbury Street 🏛️

❽ Aladin 🍴

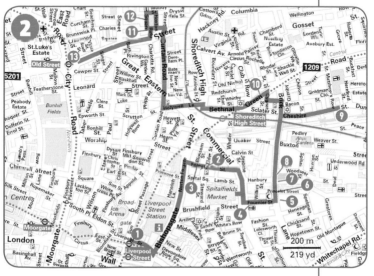

noon–10:30pm | 132 Brick Lane | tel. 72 47 82 10 | aladin bricklane.net | Budget). Continue along Brick Lane where it now gets hipper with the **Old Truman Brewery** *(www.tru manbrewery.com)*, at its epicentre, with trendy shops and bars. Browse in the designer boutiques and the **⑨ Beyond Retro** *(www.beyondretro.com)* vintage clothing emporium **on the right in Cheshire Street (no. 110–112).** Past the painted house faces and small vintage clothing shops, **go along Bethnal Green Road** to the cultural centre **⑩ Rich Mix** *(35–47 Bethnal Green Road | www.richmix.org.uk)*. Its multicultural programme reflects the area's vibes and has something to offer for the whole community: exhibitions, concerts for grown-ups and children, cinemas with cheap tickets for youngsters, theatre, comedy. **Cross Shoreditch High Street and go along Holywell Lane and Great Eastern Street before turning off right into Curtain Road. Cross Old Street; on your left-hand side, a small street leads to the green space** of **⑪ Hoxton Square**. New cafés and restaurants set up shop on the green square after the White Cube Gallery left.

05:00pm Enjoy the relaxed atmosphere around the small square over a cocktail at **⑫ Happiness Forgets → p. 85.** When you're ready, **continue along Coronet Street and follow Old Street to the right,** to the final destination of

Brick Lane: finest examples of street art

⑨ Beyond Retro

⑩ Rich Mix

⑪ Hoxton Square

⑫ Happiness Forgets

this walk, **⑬ Old Street** tube station, the epicentre of the new "Silicon Roundabout", a cluster of new technology start-ups.

⑬ Old Street

3 CULTURE, CATHEDRALS AND CULINARY DISCOVERIES ALONG THE THAMES

START: ❶ Westminster Station
END: ❶ Westminster Station

Distance:
🚶 10 km/6.2 miles

1 day
Walking time
(without stops)
2 ½ hours

COSTS: boat tour with **City Cruises** £10 (one-way trip), admissions £32, food & drink £18
WHAT TO PACK: camera

IMPORTANT TIPS: the last boat travels at 5.20pm (later in summer); departure times can vary slightly, depending on the tide. Tickets booked online for the ❹ **London Eye** are cheaper.

One of London's most beautiful strolls leads from west to east along the Thames, opening up the river panorama. London started on the north bank of the Thames; for centuries, the south bank remained its scruffier counterpart. The conversion of a power station into the Tate Modern art gallery kick-started the regeneration of this area.

10:00am Start at ❶ **Westminster Station**. The unusual, aesthetically questionable building with the vertical black bands to your left stands in strange contrast to the ensemble of the Houses of Parliament. **Portcullis House** (1999) houses MPs' offices and is ecologically sound through its energy-saving construction. ❷ **Westminster Bridge** affords sweeping views of the Thames with an amazing view to the Norman Shaw Buildings on the Victoria Embankment, a brick-red and white-banded building with tower, which was up until 1967 the headquarters of New Scotland Yard, the London metropolitan police headquarters. **Cross the bridge and turn left down the steps to the south bank.** The massive complex from the first half of the 20th century, ❸ **County Hall**, once housed London's city council; nowadays it's a place where kids have fun: **London Aquarium** (www.visitsealife.com), **The London Dungeon** (www.thedungeons.com/london) and **Shrek's Adventure** (www.shreksadventure.

❶ Westminster Station 🏛

❷ Westminster Bridge

❸ County Hall 🏛

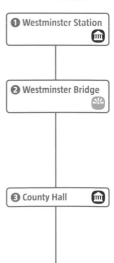

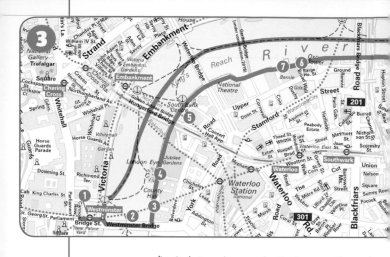

④ London Eye 🎡 🍴

⑤ South Bank Centre 🏛 🎵

⑥ OXO Tower 🛍

⑦ Pieminister 🍴

⑧ Tate Modern 🏛 🍴

⑨ Shakespeare's Globe Theatre 🏛

com/london). From here, under the huge cantilevered structure of the **④ London Eye → p. 54** you can watch the pods of the observation wheel pass by. Climb in! After your journey **continue along the banks. Adjacent to the Golden Jubilee Bridge** there's the **⑤ South Bank Centre**, a tuned-up concrete fortress from the 1950s, with the Royal Festival Hall, National Theatre, British Film Institute and Hayward Gallery. Summer often sees outdoor entertainers and free events (e.g. comedy, jazz, circus). Look over to the northern side to spot London's oldest monument, Cleopatra's Needle (approx. 1450 BC). This granite obelisk – which has nothing to do with Cleopatra bar its Egyptian origin – was set up here in 1878. **Continue along the banks** and you'll see the **⑥ OXO Tower's** OXO lettering glowing red at night. With the trick of stencilling their logo into the brick tower, the stock-cube firm circumvented a ban on riverside advertising. The viewpoint on the 8th floor is open to the public and **OXO Tower Wharf** has some interesting designer shops with fashon, art and jewellery. **In Gabriel's Wharf** try an authentic English pie from **⑦ Pieminister** *(daily 10:30am–5pm | tel. 79 28 57 55 | www.pieminister.co.uk | Budget)*.

01:00pm Further along the bank the brick tower of the **⑧ Tate Modern → p. 56** comes into sight. Go up to the 10th floor of the new annex for a great free view. A few steps further along, the timbered octagon of **⑨ Shakespeare's Globe Theatre → p. 55** was rebuilt

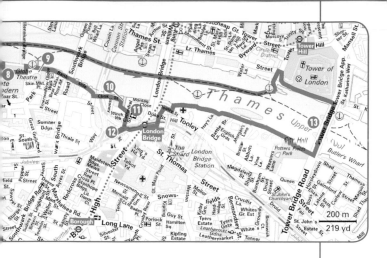

only 180 m/590 ft from its original site, true in every detail. In Shakespeare's time this was a disreputable quarter full of brothels, bear-baiting pits and gambling dens. Today the area is on the up. **Go right into Bank End and through the underpass to Clink Street** to the ⑩ **"Golden Hinde II"** *(www.goldenhinde.com)*, the replica of Francis Drake's sailing ship. **Then continue along Cathedral Street** to ⑪ **Southwark Cathedral.** Here an alabaster monument (1912) commemorates William Shakespeare, in front of a stained-glass window with characters from his works. Continue along Cathedral Street and sample your way through the gourmet food stalls of ⑫ Borough Market → p. 79. In the direction of St Thomas Street you have an excellent view of Europe's second tallest building, the unmistakable glass splinter The Shard designed by star architect Renzo Piano → p. 56. **Turn towards London Bridge and stroll right along Tooley Street and the Thames bank past the City Hall,** over the ⑬ **Tower Bridge** → p. 56 to the north bank where you can buy tickets for exhibitions in the Victorian **engine rooms** on the south bank – not just something for fans of technology. **Climb the 42 m/138 ft high pedestrian bridge,** and if you're not frightened of heights look down through the glass floor onto the Thames below, `INSIDER TIP` particularly spectacular when the moveable roadways lift for passing larger ships.

⑩ "Golden Hinde II"

⑪ Southwark Cathedral

⑫ Borough Market

⑬ Tower Bridge

① Westminster Station

05:00pm **From the Tower Millennium Pier on the north bank**, take a wonderful boat ride on the ★ **Thames** with **City Cruises** *(daily from 10am, boats every 40 min. | tel. 77 40 04 00 | www.citycruises.com)* with excellent views of London. Cross the Westminster Pier back to ① **Westminster Station**.

4 A SUNDAY STROLL FOR ANY DAY OF THE WEEK

START: ① Westminster Station END: ⑩ Kensington Palace	½ day Walking time (without stops) 2 ½ hours
Distance: ➡ 8 km/5 miles	

COSTS: Entrance ④ Wellington Arch £4.70 boat ride on ⑥ Serpentine lake £12 an hour, £10 for 30 min., admission to ⑩ Kensington Palace £16.50, food & drink £32

IMPORTANT TIPS: take the tour between April and October as otherwise the boat hire will be closed.

London's parks are popular for picnics, jogging and sunbathing. These green areas invite you to take a stroll in summer especially when the roses are blooming and you can go rowing on the Serpentine lake. The tour takes you to four of the Royal Parks in the west of London.

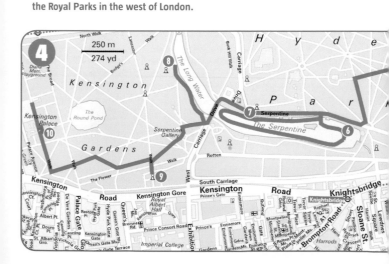

DISCOVERY TOURS

11:00am Turn right at ❶ **Westminster Station** and follow Bridge Street away from the Thames. Turn right into Parliament Street and left into King Charles Street. **Crossing Horse Guards Road,** enter ❷ **St James's Park**. To the right above the treetops look out for the bronze statue atop the granite Duke of York Column. Its lofty height led to jokes about the Duke (1763–1827) attempting to escape his creditors – at the time of his death he owed an impressive £2 million. On its northern side, the park is bounded by St James's, home to numerous gentlemen's clubs. **Cross the bridge over the pond** for a splendid view of Buckingham Palace → p. 34. **Turn left following the pond until you meet a footpath turning right in front of the Victoria Memorial. Crossing The Mall** brings you into ❸ **Green Park**, a wide expanse of lawn with fewer trees and an interesting history as a plague burial ground, hunting ground and vegetable garden during World War II. **Follow one of the paths running parallel to Constitution Hill to Hyde Park Corner; the underpass brings you to** ❹ **Wellington Arch** *(daily 10am–4pm)*. This triumphal arch used to shelter the smallest police station in London; today you can enjoy the view of, amongst other things, Apsley House designed around 1775 and boasting the fabulous address "No. 1 London" – for the first house behind London's customs barrier. This was home to the Duke of Wellington between 1817 and his death in 1852.

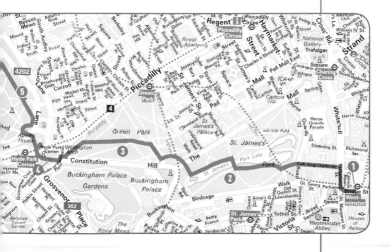

London's sun can be best soaked up in the city's Green Park

12:00pm **Through the silver-filigree Queen Elizabeth Gate behind Apsley House** step into **Hyde Park** → p. 30: 145 hectares of softly undulating lawns with clusters of old trees, flowerbeds and sculptures. **Follow Lover's Walk past the Achilles statue in the direction of Speaker's Corner.** The **5** **7 July Memorial** with 52 steel pillars commemorates the victims of the bomb attacks on 7 July, 2005. **Keep left, cross Hyde Park** in the direction of the **6** **Serpentine lake**. On the left is the **BlueBird Boats** boathouse *(boat hire April–Oct. daily. approx. 10am until sunset | tel. 72 62 19 89)*. See the park from a different perspective. After a short tour of the lake by rowing or peddle boat **carry on along the water's edge. Shortly before reaching the Serpentine Bridge** you'll come across the kiosk **7** **The Triangle** *(Budget)*. Take a well-earned break and enjoy the view over to the opposite bank with the lido and the water-filled granite oval behind the bridge: the Diana, Princess of Wales Memorial Fountain. For over 100 years, Christmas Day has seen hardy swimmers compete in the Serpentine lake for the Peter Pan Cup, formerly presented by James Matthew Barrie (1860–1937), author of the famous story about a small boy who never grew up.

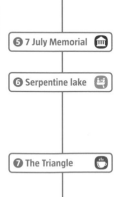

5 7 July Memorial 🏛

6 Serpentine lake 🍴

7 The Triangle ☕

`02:00pm` **When you cross the bridge and head right to the north and along the water,** you'll reach the elegant ⑧ **Peter Pan Statue**: Peter Pan with his flute surrounded by squirrels and mice. Barrie himself commissioned the sculptor G. Frampton to make the sculpture and exhibited it in 1912. **Head back to the bridge and then turn right.** This is where Hyde Park turns into **Kensington Gardens** without you noticing. **Follow the footpath in the direction of the Serpentine Gallery; if you turn right into Flower Walk,** you will see the ⑨ **Albert Memorial** → p. 29 on your left. **Turn right into Dial Walk** – ⑩ **Kensington Palace** → p. 30 is now on your left – and after the long walk and boat ride, treat yourself to a proper afternoon tea or a glass or Pimm's, the ultimate English summer drink, in the welcoming `INSIDER TIP` **Orangery** *(daily 10am–4pm | tel. 31 66 61 13 | www.orangerykensingtonpalace.co.uk | Moderate)*.

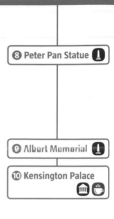

⑧ Peter Pan Statue

⑨ Albert Memorial

⑩ Kensington Palace

5 CHELSEA – AFFLUENT, MODERN, CHIC

START: ① Sloane Square Station	½ day
END: ⑧ Cadogan Hall	Walking time (without stops)
Distance: 4 km/2.5 miles	1¼ hour

COSTS: admissions £25, food & drink £30
IMPORTANT TIPS: ④ Chelsea Physic Garden and ⑤ Royal Hospital Chelsea closed Sat, Royal Hospital closed on Sundays as well, pre-book for a concert in ⑧ Cadogan Hall

Chelsea invites you to come and shop. A well-known destination is King's Road with its many boutiques and cafés. Once London's hippy quarter then the party mile of Princess Diana, this affluent district is now the home of contemporary art. On this tour you'll pass exclusive stores, historical houses, men in scarlet coats and splendid views over the Thames – a mixture of art, fashion, nature and history.

`12:00pm` From the ① **Sloane Square Station take a left into King's Road,** named after King Charles II who had the road built in his own honour. In the 1960s and 1970s it was the epicentre of the city's hippie culture where Vivienne Westwood opened her first punk fashion store. In the 1980s Chelsea became an exclusive nightspot where the

① Sloane Square Station

② Saatchi Gallery 🏛

likes of Princess Diana could be spotted. Today the quarter is home to many fashion labels, antique shops, small cafés and pubs. On the left is the world-famous **②** **Saatchi Gallery** → p. 32, which creates sensations with its contemporary art exhibitions. The exhibitions are free to the public and show what is going on in the international art scene. Stroll past the various exclusive and smaller fashion labels. **On the corner of Chelsea Manor Street** go to **Old Town Hall**, known for its antique and art trade fairs. **Continue left into Oakley Street which merges into the elegant pastel-coloured Royal Albert Bridge,** re-opened in 2011 after an expensive refurbishment. **Turn left before the bridge** into the famous **③** **Cheyne Walk** → p. 30, once the home of famous and illustrious personalities – blue plaques on the houses indicate who once lived there for example the writer Henry James in no. 21, painter Dante Gabriel Rossetti in no. 16, novelist George Eliot in no. 4 and in no. 3 the Rolling Stones' guitarist Keith Richards. At the end of the road, keep right and continue your route left along the Chelsea Embankment.

③ Cheyne Walk 🏛

④ Chelsea Physic Garden 🌳 🍴

02:00pm You'll now reach the outskirts of the **④** **Chelsea Physic Garden** → p. 30, **take a left into Swan Walk to enter the gardens.** Stroll between the medicinal plants in this apothecary garden and enjoy a refreshing break in

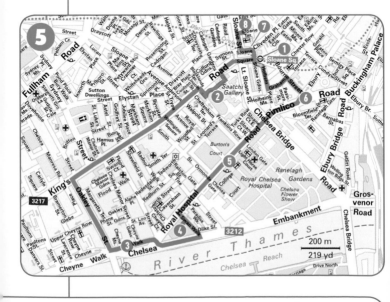

the garden's café **Tangerine Dream Café** *(tel. 73 49 64 64 | Budget)*. **The route now continues along the Royal Hospital Road.** Don't be surprised if you're met by friendly men in scarlet coats. Close by is the ❺ **Royal Hospital Chelsea** *(Mon–Fri 10am–4pm | donations requested | www.chelsea-pensioners.co.uk)*, the residential home for pensioned British soldiers erected in 1692 from plans drawn up by Sir Christopher Wren. Enter the well-maintained building and its *Great Hall* with the country's military history carved into the wooden panelling on the walls. Take a look at the chapel opposite and in the park gardens towards the Thames. The famous *Chelsea Flower Show* is held here every May, a major event in the British gardeners' calendar. **The route carries on along Pimlico Road to** ❻ **Orange Square**. Take a sweet break here with **INSIDERTIP** hot chocolate at **R Chocolate** *(198 Ebury Street)* and think about returning on Saturday to people-watch at the small exclusive farmer's market where you can buy local products such as fish from Kent or fresh pesto with homemade pasta.

London Jazz Festival in Cadogan Hall

05:00pm Finish your day with an evening meal and a concert. **Return to Sloane Square which you then cross.** ❼ **Côte** *(daily 7am–1pm, pre-theatre menu noon–7pm | 7–12 Sloane Square | tel. 78 81 59 99 | www.cote-restaurants.co.uk | Budget)* offers a special theatre menu. After a good meal, **go around the square and turn right into Sloane Street until you reach Sloane Terrace on your right.** Here is the ❽ **Cadogan Hall** → p. 88, all types of concerts are held here every evening at 7pm: from guitar concerts, the Philharmonic Orchestra to the London Jazz Festival.

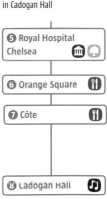

❺ Royal Hospital Chelsea

❻ Orange Square

❼ Côte

❽ Cadogan Hall

TRAVEL WITH KIDS

Exploring London with children in tow? Sounds exhausting. But do not despair: there are lots of things to do with kids, from toddler to teenager. *Visit London* has an excellent section with information on all kinds of activities: *www.visit london.com/things-to-do/activities/ family-activities.*

the *Tower of London* (p. 50)? If you book several attractions in one go you get a discount, also for family tickets. In Leavesden, about half an hour away from London, you can immerse yourself in the world of Harry Potter by visiting the film sets of *Warner Brothers Studios (www. wbstudiotour.co.uk).*

INDOOR

A true blessing for familys on a tight budget are the museums that are free of charge. The *Science Museum* (p. 33) has a water and light show that young children will love while the older ones can have fun with the interactive experiments. *The Natural History Museum* (p. 31) even lets the whole family spend the night among dinosaurs. *Country Hall* (p. 107) has several attractions to offer: in the *Sea Life London Aquarium* you come face to face with big and small fish. *The London Dungeon* (for children aged 12 years and over) will give teenagers thrills and a good fright. *Shrek's Adventure* (6 years and over) promises a magical journey with special effects. If you want to meet your favourite celebrities, visit *Madame Tussauds* wax museum (p. 58). Or would you rather play knights and princesses in

OUTDOOR

There's a tingly feeling in your tummy when the glass capsule of the giant ferris wheel London Eye (p. 54) starts to ascend into the sky! A guided tour on Sir Francis Drake's pirate ship *"Golden Hinde II"* (p. 109) is also very exciting. Places to romp and play in are the *Diana Memorial Playground* (139 D1) *(\U0001D4DD C7)* in Kensington Gardens with pirate ship and the *adventure playground in Battersea Park* (0) *(\U0001D4DD F12) (southwestern corner)* with sand pit, slides and climbing ropes. Typical city dwellers like monkeys, tigers, hippopotami, penguins and giraffes can be found in the *London Zoo* (132 B–C1) *(\U0001D4DD F–G2) (www.zsl. org/zsl-london-zoo).* The journey there turns into an adventure if you arrive at the zoo by *London Waterbus (www. londonwaterbus.com),* from "Little Ven-

As a versatile and green large city, London has much to offer kids – not only museums and the zoo

ice" via the Regent's Canal. Travelling on the Thames by boat is also great fun – you can do this on boats and ferries that are included in your city tour tickets (p. 125) or in one of the yellow amphibian vehicles of *London Duck Tours (www. londonducktours.co.uk)*. Riding out to *Queen Elizabeth Olympic Park* (p. 59) on the DLR that runs without a driver (p. 125) is quite a surreal feeling; in the park younger kids can shoot down the slide at *Arcelor Mittal Orbit* while the older ones try their hand at *Urban Mountaineering* by walking over the roof of the *O₂ Arena* (0) (*ⓂＬ O*) in Greenwich 52 m/171 ft above ground with climbing gear and helmet *(children must to be at least 10 years old or 1.20 m/4 ft tall | www.theo2. co.uk/do-more-at-the-o2/up-at-the-o2).*

SHOPPING & FOOD

M&M's World at Leicester Square **(134 A6)** (*ⓂＬ I6*) is all about those colourful chocolate treats whereas across the street at

Lego the plastic building stones abound. An absolute must-see is *Hamley's* **(133 E6)** (*ⓂＬ H6*), the largest toy shop in the country with toys of every kind on several floors! From there it's only a short walk to Oxford Street which will have teenage shoppers shouting for joy.

The cafés of the big museums frequently offer a children's menu and some even have a picnic area where you can bring your own food. You can check how child-friendly a place is, by asking for a high chair. Children are not really welcome in pubs; it is actually against the law to take them into bar areas or into pubs in general during the evening. Good places to go to with children are *Pizza Pilgrims* (p. 66), *Wahaca* **(134 A6)** (*ⓂＬ K6*) *(66 Chandos Place | www.wahaca.co.uk)* which serves Mexican food, *Tom's Kitchen* **(144 C1)** (*ⓂＬ Q6*) *(1 Commodity Quay | www.tomskitchen.co.uk)* and on a Sunday afternoon the *Brasserie Zédel* (p. 68). Also look out for places advertised as *family restaurants*.

FESTIVALS & EVENTS

Londoners care about tradition, ritual and splendid uniforms, and not only the royals know how to play the gallery. As varied as the diverse cultures living in London are their festivities which they open up to a wide audience. Consult the *Time Out* listings magazine (every Tuesday, *www.timeout.com/london*).

EVENTS

JANUARY

1 Jan *London Parade:* Annual parade on the the streets of the West End with lots of marching bands from the US. New Year, noon from Hotel Ritz; *www.london parade.co.uk*

JANUARY/FEBRUARY

INSIDER TIP *Chinese New Year:* This festival is traditionally celebrated with dragon parades and dancing; the date varies each year, 2018: 16th Feb., 2019: 5th Feb; *www.londonchinatown.org*

MARCH

17 March *St Patrick's Day:* The Irish patron saint is drank to; on the Sunday nearest to the date: parade and festival on Trafalgar Square; *www.visit london.com*

APRIL

London Marathon: 40,000 runners, some in crazy costumes raising money for charity; *www.virginmoneylondonmara thon.com*

MAY

Late May *Chelsea Flower Show:* important high-society flower and garden exhibition; *www.rhs.org.uk*

JUNE

2nd or 3rd Sat *Trooping the Colour:* birthday parade for Queen Elizabeth II in Horse Guards Parade; *www.trooping-the-colour.co.uk*
From late June *Wimbledon Lawn Tennis Championships:* renowned international tennis tournament; *www.wimbledon.com*

JULY

Mid-July–mid-Sept ★ *Promenade Concerts (Proms):* classical music in the Royal Albert Hall; *www.bbc.co.uk/proms*

AUGUST

Early Aug *Great British Beer Festival:* featuring 500 *ales* and *ciders*, Earls Court; *www.gbbf.org.uk*
Late Sun/Mon: ★ *Notting Hill Carnival:*

Caribbean street carnival in the middle of summer, with colourful parade and flamboyant costumes; *thelondonnottinghill carnival.com*

SEPTEMBER
INSIDER TIP *The Mayor's Thames Festival:* London's greatest outdoor arts festival with events around the Thames, plus a night carnival; *totallythames.org.*
Great River Race: race of 300 traditional boats – 21 miles from Richmond to Greenwich; *www.greatriverrace.co.uk.*
London Design Festival: 10-day high-class event at the V&A Museum and more places; *www.londondesignfestival.com*

OCTOBER
1st Sun *Pearly Queens:* harvest festival of the market traders in costumes embossed with a myriad of mother-of-pearl buttons, St Paul's Church, Covent Garden; *www. pearlysociety.co.uk*
Mid–late Oct *London Film Festival: www. bfi.org.uk/lff*

NOVEMBER
5 Nov/nearest weekend: *Bonfire Night:* fireworks commemorating Guy Fawkes' failed attempt to blow up Parliament in 1605

2nd Sat *Lord Mayor's Show:* procession inducting the new Mayor of the City of London; *lordmayorsshow.london*
Mid-Nov. *Jazz Festival:* 10 days of the finest improvised jazz. International musicians play throughout the city; *www. visitlondon.com*

DECEMBER
Evening *Christmas carol singing* on Trafalgar Square. On 31 December much of London sees in the New Year here

NATIONAL HOLIDAYS

1 Jan	New Year's Day
March/April	Good Friday; Easter Monday
1st Mon in May	*Bank Holiday*
last Mon in May	*Bank Holiday*
last Mon in Aug	*Bank Holiday*
25/26 Dec	Christmas

If 1 Jan or 25/26 Dec is a Saturday or Sunday, the holiday falls on the following workday.

LINKS, BLOGS, APPS & MORE

www.derelictlondon.com The author used his long walks to photograph the surprising beauty of the crumbling and unloved London behind the tourist facades: another proof that you discover so much more when you're walking. Also available in book form

www.curiocity.org.uk Creating curious maps of London, for example *London Dissected:* London as a giant sprawling body composed of arterial thoroughfares,

intestinal subways, nervous wiring and lymphatic waterways. Or how about *London Bestiary* to go on the hunt for the city's wild animals? Maps available from £5 in the online shop

www.londonslostrivers.com A beautiful collection of lost and well-known rivers in London; photos, historical facts and explanations provide a special insight. Even better: a guided tour of the city by the author Paul Telling

http://londonist.com This page offers events listings, fun photographs, a WiFi map of London, and much more

www.streetartlondon.co.uk Graffiti, spray and stencils – this page helps you keep abreast of a quickly changing scene; an app navigates you to the most beautiful works

www.littleobservationist.com Blog from a New York-born woman living in London since 2007 who shares her views and opinions on art and design, shops and bars, city walks and tips

www.run-riot.com Selected news from London's underground and hip culture, with weekly indie music podcast

www.spottedbylocals.com Real Londoners share the pearls they find – restaurants, markets, shops – with the online community, displaying remarkable enthusiasm. Also available as an app

Regardless of whether you are still preparing your trip or already in London: these addresses will provide you with more information, videos and networks to make your holiday even more enjoyable.

http://londonbloggers.iamcal.com This page unites over 4,000 London blogs – occasionally filled with curses about London's public transport system

http://london-underground.blogspot. com Video clips and pictures of day-to-day life on the London tube; a thankful and sheer inexhaustible theme

www.couchsurfing.org Internet-based community for free stays with locals. The emphasis is on cultural exchange rather than on freeloading. The various sub-groups can take care of your social life too

VIDEOS & MUSIC

http://www.soundsurvey.org.uk/ The sounds and sonic background of London Town, constantly updated!

http://www.youtube.com/watch?v=QOXvxBM7hJI Four "business ninjas" in suits run parkour – the urban free-running style – across various obstacles to get to their place of work in the City

short.travel/lon17 Historical film footage (from as far back as 1890!) with map details and comparison with photos of London today show how the city has changed and what has remained the same

APPS

Smart Parents This app gives parents event tips for children: *hoop.co.uk*

London Cycle Free London bike hire app shows you the nearest station and bike availability in real time

Check in Easy When you reach a certain age, you don't want the hassle of waiting out in the cold to gain admission to places. Use the guest list & event check in Manager App to get your name entered on the guest list at top clubs. Free service

TRAVEL TIPS

ARRIVAL

🚗 If you're travelling by car: the M25 is the motorway orbiting London, the *North Circular* (A406)/*South Circular* (A205) the inner ring road.

🚆 Trains from other British cities should be booked with the maximum advance to take advantage of good prices; Britain has one of Europe's priciest railways. *www.nationalrail.co.uk*

✈ Scheduled flights generally land in Heathrow *(www.heathrow.com)*, 18 km/11 miles west of the city centre, most budget carriers either in Stansted (northeast; *www.stanstedairport.com*), Luton (north; *www.london-luton.co.uk*) or Gatwick (south; *www.gatwickairport.com*). Business flyers also use the very central London City Airport *(www.london cityairport.com)* in East London.

RESPONSIBLE TRAVEL

While traveling you can influence a lot. Don't just keep track of your carbon footprint *(www.myclimate.org)* by planning an ecologically harmless route. Also think about how you can protect nature and culture abroad *(www.ecotrans.org)*. It is all the more important that as a tourist you take into consideration aspects such as the conservation of nature *(www.wwf.org)*, regional products, minimal use of cars, saving water and many more things. For more information on ecological tourism look at *www.ecotourism.org*.

Buses *(including: www.nationalexpress.com)* serve all airports, e.g. from Stansted to Victoria (90 min.): from £18 return. Bus Stansted–Baker St. or Victoria *(www.easybus.co.uk)* £4–16 return.

By tube (Piccadilly Line), the trip from Heathrow to the city centre takes just under an hour (give yourself more time on the way back to the airport, to allow for delays!), by Heathrow-Express to Paddington (£36 return) only 15 min.

From other airports: Gatwick Express (train, 30 min.) to Victoria £35.50 return, online £31.60; Stansted Express (train, 45 min., £28 return) to/from Liverpool Street; Luton: e.g. bus one way **INSIDER TIP** booked online from £2 *(www.easybus.co.uk, online discounts apply to other services too)*!

🛳 From Ireland, the ferry from Dun Laoghaire, Cork or Belfast is a convenient way to travel, with competitive pricing. Dun Laoghaire–Holyhead takes 100 minutes with HSS; Dublin–Holyhead 3¾ hours or under 2 hours on the fast ferry. Rosslare–Fishguard 4 hours; Cork–Swansea 10 hours. From Holyhead or Fishguard it is about a 6-hour drive to London, about 5 hours from Swansea. Compare prices and times: Irish Ferries *(www.irishferries.com)*, Stena Lines *(www.stenaline.com)*, Brittany Ferries *(www.brittanyferries.com)*.

BIKING

24 hours a day, seven days a week, tourists too may use the robust aluminium bikes with three gears. ⬤ Short trips under 30 minutes are free! Take your

From arrival to weather

VISA or MasterCard to the nearest docking station – in the city centre there is one every 400–500 m/1,310–1,640 ft, recognisable by the words CYCLE HIRE or a blue version of the tube symbol – and follow the simple instructions to release a bike. The net is constantly being extended.

CONSULATES & EMBASSIES

EMBASSY OF THE UNITED STATES
(132 C3) (*∅ G8*) | 24 Grosvenor Square | uk.usembassy.gov | tel. 74 99 90 00 | tube Bond Street or Marble Arch (Central)

EMBASSY OF CANADA
(132 C3) (*∅ F–G8*) | 1 Grosvenor Square | canada.embassyhomepage.com | tel. 72 58 66 00 | tube Bond Street or Marble Arch (Central)

EMBASSY OF IRELAND
(140 B4) (*∅ F5*) | 17 Grosvenor Place | www.embassyofireland.co.uk | tel. 72 35 21 71 | tube Hyde Park Corner (Piccadilly)

CUSTOMS

The allowance when entering Great Britain from countries outside the European Union, including North America, is: 1 litre of spirits, 200 cigarettes or 100 cigarillos or 50 cigars or 250 g of tobacco, 50 g of perfume or 250 g of eau de toilette and other articles (except gold) to a value of £390.

Note that the import of self-defence sprays is prohibited and the import of other weapons requires licences. For more information: www.hmrc.gov.uk/customs

DRIVING

Travellers should bear in mind that Britain drives on the left; at roundabouts cars coming from the right have the right of way. Cameras monitoring speed limits are usually obvious: normally 30 mp/h (50 km/h). Driving in the city centre Mon–Fri 7am–6pm incurs an automatic congestion charge (£11.50 | tfl.gov.uk/modes/driving/congestion-charge | tel. 0343 2 22 22 22 [*]). Automobile Association (AA) (emergency tel. 0800 88 77 55 | www.theaa.com). For cheap car rentals try www.easycar.com.

ELECTRICITY

Voltage: 240 Volt/50 Hz. Power points/plugs are three-pin and often have an on/off switch. Bring an adapter if you are not from Britain!

EMERGENCY SERVICES

The central emergency number 999 will get you a switchboard for ambulance, fire services and the police.

HEALTH

EU citizens are still entitled to free emergency treatment in hospital. Remember to bring your EHIC insurance card. This should also be your first port of call for not immediately life-threatening but urgent conditions (Accident & Emergency, A & E – 24-hour e.g. St Mary's (131 F5) (*∅ D5*) (Praed St. tel. 33 12 66 66 | tube Paddington), otherwise a general practitioner working in the state-run National Health Service, NHS, e.g. NHS Walk-In

Clinics *(133 F5)* *(∅ J5)* *(1 Frith St. | tel. 75 34 65 00).* 24-hour pharmacy: *Zafash (139 D5)(∅ C10) (233 Old Brompton Road | tel. 73 73 27 98 | www.zafash. co.uk | tube District, Piccadilly: Earls Court).* Prescription-free medication is available in the stores of drugstore chain *Boots.* Emergency dentist (payable): *Barts and The London Dental Hospital (137 D4)(∅ R5) (Turner St. | tel. 77 67 32 03 (during the day) | 35 94 09 38 (evenings and on weekends) | tube District: Whitechapel).* North American citizens should bring proof of their travel health insurance.

INFORMATION

ww.visitbritain.com, www.visitlondon. com, www.londononline.co.uk, www.lon dontourist.org, www.londontown.com, www.timeout.com

CITY OF LONDON INFORMATION CENTRE

(135 E5) (∅ N5–6)
Mon–Sat 9:30am–5:30pm, Sun 10am–4pm | St Paul's Churchyard | tel. 73 32 14 56 | www.visitthecity.co.uk | tube Central: St Paul's, Circle, District: Blackfriars

HOLBORN INFORMATION KIOSK

(134 B4–5) (∅ K5)
Mon–Fri 8am–6pm | 88–94 Kingsway | outside Holborn tube station | tube Central, Piccadilly: Holborn

INTERNET & WIFI

By now, you can get free WiFi almost everywhere in the city; less so outside the city. Many coffee shops and pubs offer free WiFi hotspots; hotels often charge for the service. There's also WiFi in more than 250 tube stations. A WiFi pass costs

SPOTLIGHT ON SPORTS

Fancy worshipping at the altar of the national god: football (soccer)? Tickets for Premier League matches involving iconic clubs like Arsenal *(www.arsenal. com)*, Chelsea *(www.chelseafc.com)* and Tottenham Hotspurs *(www.totten hamhotspur.com)* are difficult to get hold of – try *www.viagogo.com*. Another option is to contact smaller clubs such as Crystal Palace *(www.cpfc. co.uk)*, Fulham *(www.fulhamfc.com)*, West Ham United *(www.whufc.com)*; you won't be lacking for atmosphere. Or take a tour through Wembley Stadium (Norman Foster's new edition) *(0) (∅ 0). Tel. 0800 8 00 27 55 (*) | www.wembleystadium.com | tube Metropolitan: Wembley Park*

You can't get much more English than cricket. *Lord's Cricket Ground (131 F2) (∅ D3) (St John's Wood Road | tickets: tel. 74 32 10 00 | guided tours: daily 10am, 11am, noon, 2pm | £20 | tel. 76 16 85 95 | www.lords.org | tube Jubilee: St John's Wood).* If you like it a bit rougher: Twickenham Stadium *(0) (∅ 0) (Tickets: tel. 0871 2 22 20 20)* is the London home of rugby. *Museum of Rugby (Tue–Sat 10am–5pm, Sun 11am–5pm | guided tours: Tue–Sat 11am, 1pm, 3pm, Sun 10:30am, noon, 1:30pm, 3pm (except match days) | £20 | Whitton Road | Twickenham | tel. 88 92 88 77 | www.englandrugby.com/ twickenham/world-rugby-museum | trains: Twickenham, from Waterloo).*

£2/day or £5/week or is free if you are a Virgin customer *(my.virginmedia.com/wifi/)*.

LOST & FOUND

For insurance reasons, stolen items should be reported to the police. For items lost on the tube/bus/black cabs: *Transport For London Lost Property Office* (132 B3) *(ᗕ F4) (Mon–Fri 8:30am–4pm | tel. 0343 2 22 12 34 (*) | tfl.gov.uk/help-and-contact/lost-property | 200 Baker Street | tube Baker Street)*

CURRENCY CONVERTER

$	£	£	$
1	0.76	1	1.33
3	2.27	3	3.99
5	3.78	5	6.64
13	9.82	13	17.28
40	30.23	40	53.16
75	57	75	100
120	91	120	159
250	189	250	332
500	378	500	665

For current exchange rates see www.xe.com

PHONE & MOBILE PHONE

Telephone booths – very few of the old red ones are left – take credit cards and/or coins.

The dialling code for Britain is 0044 from Ireland and Europe, 01144 from North America; leave out the first zero of the 020 London code. To reach the US and Canada from London, dial 001, Ireland: 00 353. Operator: 100. Within London only dial the last 8 digits of the number, from a mobile/cell prefix with 020. Mobile/cell numbers start with a (0), which you leave out when calling from abroad.

At *Carphone Warehouse (daily | 434 Strand)* near Trafalgar Square you can buy SIM cards from different phone companies (£10 incl. credit). You will find a free recharging station at the green solar phone booth on Tottenham Court Road.

POST

Postcards/letters up to 20 g within Europe: £1.05. Central post office (134 A6) *(ᗕ K6) (24–28 William IV St. | Mon–Fri 8:30am–6.:0pm, Sat 9am–5:30pm | tube Bakerloo, Northern: Charing Cross)*

PRICES

Travellers from abroad can change money commission-free into pound sterling, in day-to-day language *quid*, in larger post offices.

Taking money out from an ATM/cash point, may incur a fee. VISA and Master-Card are widespread.

PUBLIC TRANSPORT

The best source of information is *www.tfl.gov.uk*. The underground, *tube*, runs on twelve colour-coded lines, plus the DLR *(Docklands Light Railway)*. A day *Travelcard*, valid on buses too, is nearly always the best option, zones 1–2 for the centre, zones 1–6 (£12.10 from 9:30am). Check which zone your hotel is in when booking! Or buy a *Visitor Oystercard* (many fares up to 50 per cent reduced). You can buy it in advance at www.visitbritainshop.com, credits from £20.10, plus a £3 fee, rechargeable. With both cards, you can use public transport all day and you will only be charged up to a specified amount. Any leftover credit on the card under £10 is refunded by ticket machines. If you plan a longer stay in London, buy an Oystercard and charge it for a week or a month. Some credit cards can be used for touch-free payment in the tube and in buses (fees for foreign credit cards). Finally the tube also runs at night, but only on Fri/Sat. Or you can take the night buses (N) for example from/to Trafalgar Square. *24-hour London Travel Information (tel. 0343 2 22 12 34 [*])*. Travel Information Centres: train stations Liverpool Street, Victoria, Heathrow Airport.

TAXIS

The city's reliable *black cabs* (these days often in other colours) are not cheap, but you will not be taken advantage of. If the FOR HIRE/TAXI sign is lit up, the cab is free. Order a taxi through *Dial-a-cab (credit card prebookings) | tel. 72 53 50 00 | www.dialacab.co.uk)*. Minicabs: *Addison Lee (tel. 74 07 90 00 | www.ad disonlee.com), Pink Ladies Taxi Company (tel. 0843 2 08 74 65 | www.pinkladies. co.uk)* with female drivers (register online first).

TIME

Greenwich Mean Time is shared with Ireland. The North American east coast is 5 hours behind, the west coast 8 hours.

TIPS

In restaurants give 10–15 per cent. This may already be included as a service charge (check!). You never tip in pubs. Hotel porters: £1 per item of luggage.

TOURS

● Open-top red double-decker buses run on three routes. Buy tickets (valid for

WEATHER IN LONDON

	Jan	Feb	March	April	May	June	July	Aug	Sept	Oct	Nov	Dec
Daytime temperatures in °C/°F												
	6/43	7/45	10/50	13/55	17/63	20/68	22/72	21/70	19/66	14/57	10/50	7/45
Nighttime temperatures in °C/°F												
	2/36	2/36	3/37	5/41	8/46	11/52	13/55	13/55	11/52	8/46	5/41	3/37
☀ Sunshine hours/day	2	2	4	6	7	7	7	6	5	3	2	1
☂ Precipitation days/month	11	9	8	8	8	8	9	9	9	9	10	9

24 hours) from the driver (£30), online (from £26) at *www.theoriginaltour.com* or in person at 17–19 Cockspur St. Live commentary or recorded content: *Big Bus Company (www.bigbus.co.uk | online from £23 or from the bus staff | tel. 72 33 95 33)*. Both providers include a river trip.

INSIDER TIP Discover the Thames on a kayak – from Windsor or Hampton Court or on the Regent's Canal, for pros and beginners, also with a glass of champagne: *London Kayak Tours (tel. 0845 4 53 20 02 | www.londonkayaktours.co.uk)*.

City Cruises (see p. 110) take a lovely sightseeing route on the Thames (from £12.70).

INSIDER TIP Guided bike tours (daily 10:30am, £24.95, 3 hours, with registration): *London Bicycle Tour Company | www.londonbicycle.com | 1a Gabriel's Wharf | 56 Upper Ground | tel. 79 28 68 38 | tube Jubilee: Southwark.*

There are many different guided tours on foot. *London Walks (www.walks.com)* offers, for example, tours of different quarters such as Soho or Hampstead, a Beatles Walk, wartime or literature walks as well as their famous Jack the Ripper Tours and Ghost Walks at night. The *Museum of London (www.museumoflondon.org.uk)* also has a walk programme with topics like "Roman London" or "Docklands". *Britmovietours (britmovietours.com)* spe-

BUDGETING

Coffee	£3.50	for a sit-down small latte at a coffee shop
Beer	£4.60	for a pint (approx. 0.5 l) at the pub
Fish & chips	£9	at a snack counter
Cinema	£20	for a ticket
Taxi	£10.50	for a mile

cialises in film-themed walks and bus rides (Sherlock Holmes, James Bond, Doctor Who ...). The guides from *Alternative London (www.alternativeldn.co.uk)* know their way around the East End – join them on a bicycle tour or a street art walk. There are tours for birdwatchers and for photographers – and even a "loo tour" with insights into London's history of health and hygiene *(lootours.com)*.

Several operators such as *Free Tours of London (www.freetoursoflondon.com)* or *Free London Walking Tours (www.freelondonwalkingtours.com)* even offer free tours and pub crawls on a "pay what it's worth" basis.

STREET ATLAS

The green line indicates the Discovery Tour "London at a glance"
The blue line indicates the other Discovery Tours
All tours are also marked on the pull-out map

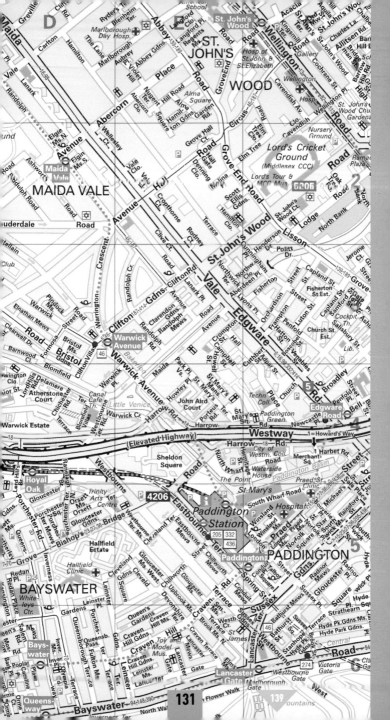

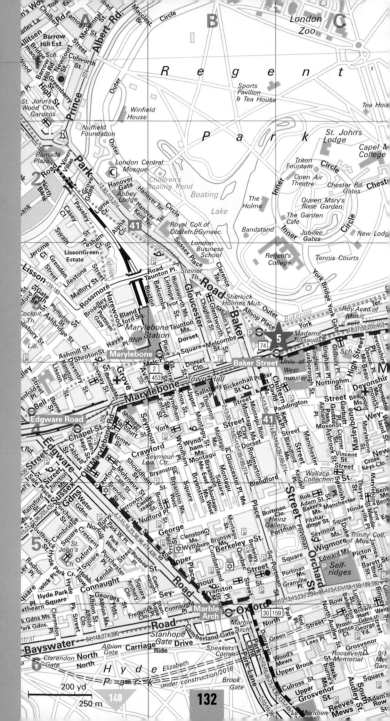

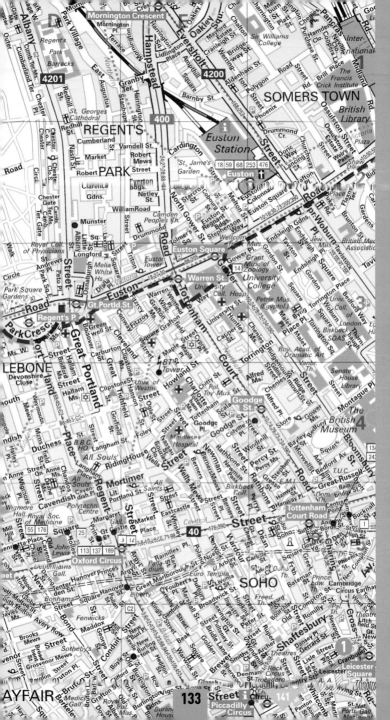

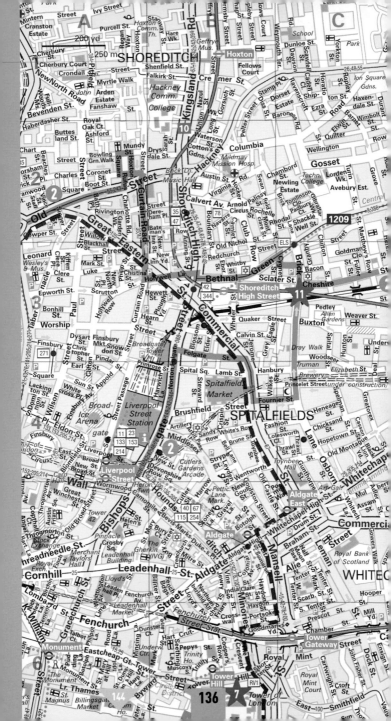

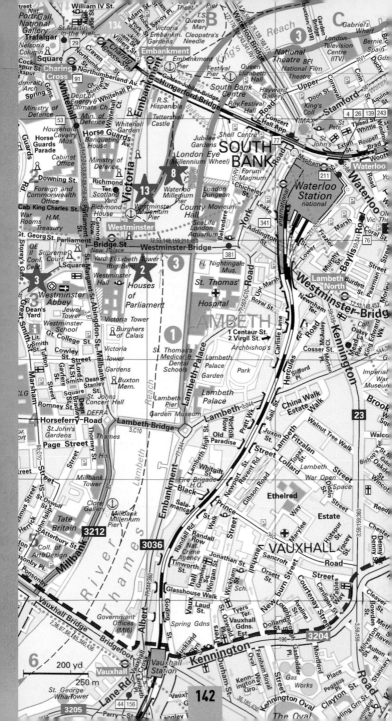

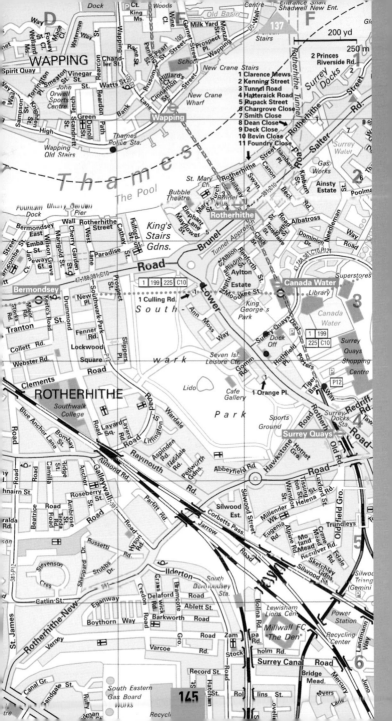

200 yd

250 m

WAPPING

Dock

King
Ms.

Woods

Old Basin

Centre

Entrance Shaft
Shadwell New Ent.

Milk Yard

New Crane Stairs

1 Clarence Mews
2 Kenning Street
3 Tunnel Road
4 Hatteraick Road
5 Rupack Street
6 Chargrove Close
7 Smith Close
8 Dean Close
9 Deck Close
10 Bevin Close
11 Foundry Close

2 Princes
Riverside Rd.

Rotherhithe Tunnel

Surrey
Docks

Spirit Quay

Way

Welland St.
Fowey Cl.

Waterman Way

Smeaton
St.

Vinegar
St.

John
Orwell
Sports
Centre

Watts
St.

Prusom
St.

Cinnamon
St.

Prospect
Pl.

Monza
St.

New Wapping

School

New Crane
Wharf

St. Mary
Ch.

Bubble
Theatre

Elephant
Lane

Mayflower
St.

Rotherhithe

Brunel Rd.

Tunnel Approach

Albatross

Needleman

Dominion
Dr.

Way

Road

Surrey
Water

Gas
Works

Ainsty
Estate

Poolma

High

St.

Green
Path

Reardon
St.

Bank

Wapping
Old Stairs

Thames
Police Sta.

Wapping

Hilliard's
Street

Cannon

Swan Rd.

Salter Rd.

Rd.

T h a m e s

The Pool

Fountain
Dock

Cherry Garden
Pier

Bermondsey
East

Wall

Rotherhithe
Street

Cathay St.

King's
Stairs
Gdns.

Marigold St.

Cherry
Garden
St.

West
Lane

Paradise
St.

Rotherhithe

Brunel Rd.

Aylton

Estate

Redriff
St.

Surrey
Water

Albatross Rd.

Canada Water

Library

Superstores

Canada
Water

Surrey
Quays
Shopping
Centre

Road

Bermondsey

1 199 225 C10

Keeto's
Road

New Pl.

Drummond

Prospect St.

1 Culling Rd.

South-

Fenner Rd.

Lockwood

Square

Ann Moss Way

Lower Road

King
George's
Park

Moodkee St.

Surrey Quays

Dock
Off

Hothfield Pl.

Porters

1 199
225 C10

Tranton

Collett Rd.

Webster Rd.

Clements

Road

ROTHERHITHE

Southwalk
College

w a r k

Seven Isl.
Leisure Ctr.

Lido

Cafe
Gallery

Park

Sports
Ground

Tiger
Bay

P12

1 Orange Pl.

Surrey
Docks
Sta.

Redriff
Rd.

Old Rd.

Surrey Quays

Blue Anchor Lane

Bombay St.

Anchor

Galleywall Road

Almond Rd.

Layard Rd.

Lynton

Aspinden
Rd.

Reddale

Wardale

Ravensbourne

Pedworth
Gdns.

Abbeyfield Rd.

Hawkstone Road

Hornet

Warndon
St.

Tissington
St. St. Helena Rd.

Road

Beatrice
Road

Ambrose
St.

Roseberry
Road

Camilla

Rossetti
Rd.

Stubbs
Dr.

Stevenson
Cres.

Catlin St.

Sheppard Dr.

Eganway

Boythorn Way

Delaford
Road

Ilderton

Barkworth

Bramcote

Road

Brunswick
Road

South
Bermondsey
Sta.

Ablett St.

Road

Silwood
Est.

Parfitt Rd.

Jarrow

Corbetts Pass.

Silwood Street

Eugenia
Rd.

Millpond
Wk.

Alpine Rd.

Mo
land
Mead
St.

Crane
Mead

Sketchley
Gdns.

Old Kent Road

Trundleys

Recuiver Rd.

Silwood St.

Silwood
Triangle
(Gemini)

St. James

Rotherhithe New

Verney

Canal Gr.

Sandgate St.

South Eastern
Gas Board
Works

Varcoe
Rd.

Record St.

Zam
pa
Rd.

holm Rd.

Lewisham
Lions Cen.

**Millwall FC
"The Den"**

Power
Station

Recycling
Center

Surrey Canal

Bridge
Mead.

Rollins St.

Road

Mercury

Juno

Landmann

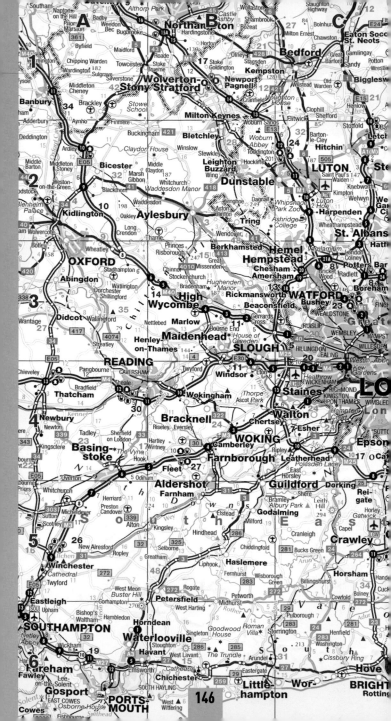

146

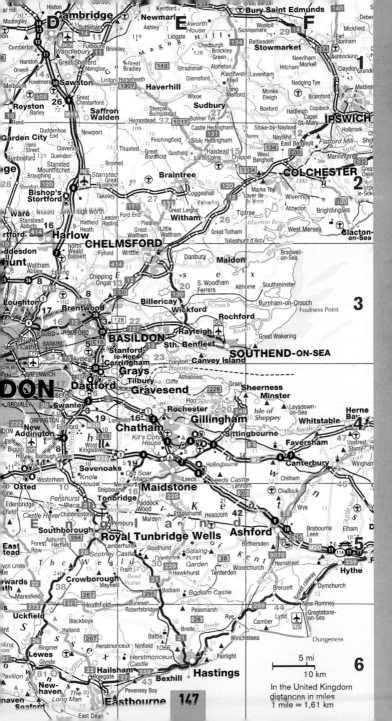

This index lists a selection of the streets and squares shown in the street atlas

Motorway Autobahn		Autoroute Autosnelweg
Road with four lanes Vierspurige Straße		Route à quatre voies Weg met vier rijstroken
Through road Durchgangsstraße		Route de transit Weg voor doorgaand verkeer
Main road Hauptstraße		Route principale Hoofdweg
Other roads Sonstige Straßen		Autres routes Overige wegen
Information - Parking Information - Parkplatz	**i** **P**	Information - Parking Informatie - Parkeerplaats
One way road Einbahnstraße	→ →	Rue à sens unique Straat met eenrichtingverkeer
Pedestrian zone Fußgängerzone		Zone piétonne Voetgangersgebied
Main railway with station Hauptbahn mit Bahnhof	▬■▬	Chemin de fer principal avec gare Belangrijke spoorweg met station
Other railways Sonstige Bahnen		Autres lignes Overige spoorwegen
Underground U-Bahn	• • • ⊖ • • •	Métro Ondergrondse spoorweg
Bus-route Buslinie	●	Ligne d'autobus Buslijn
Landing place Anlegestelle	⚓	Embarcadère Aanlegplaats
Church - Church of interest - Synagogue Kirche - Sehenswerte Kirche - Synagoge	⊞ ⊟ ▣	Église - Église remarquable - Synagogue Kerk - Bezienswaardige kerk - Synagoge
Post office - Police station Postamt - Polizei	✉ ●	Bureau de poste - Police Postkantoor - Politie
Monument - Tower Denkmal - Turm	☖ ♂	Monument - Tour Monument - Toren
Hospital - Hotel - Youth hostel Krankenhaus - Hotel - Jugendherberge	⊕ H ▲	Hôpital - Hôtel - Auberge de jeunesse Ziekenhuis - Hotel - Jeugdherberg
Built-up area - Public buildings Bebauung - Öffentliche Gebäude		Zone bâtie - Bâtiments public Woongebied - Openbaar gebouw
Industrial area Industriegebiet		Zone industrielle Industriekomplex
Park, forest - Cemetery Park, Wald - Friedhof	+ + + +	Parc, bois - Cimetière Park, bos - Begraafsplaats
Restricted traffic zone Zone mit Verkehrsbeschränkungen	▭ ▬ ▬ ▭	Circulation réglementée par des péages Zone met verkeersbeperkingen
MARCO POLO Discovery Tour 1 MARCO POLO Erlebnistour 1		MARCO POLO Tour d'aventure 1 MARCO POLO Avontuurlijke Route 1
MARCO POLO Discovery Tours MARCO POLO Erlebnistouren		MARCO POLO Tours d'aventure MARCO POLO Avontuurlijke Routes
MARCO POLO Highlight	★**1**	MARCO POLO Highlight

FOR YOUR NEXT TRIP...

MARCO POLO TRAVEL GUIDES

The travel guides with **Insider Tips**

INDEX

This index lists all sights and destinations, plus some important streets, squares, names and keywords featured in this guide. Numbers in bold indicate a main entry.

CREDITS

WRITE TO US

e-mail: info@marcopologuides.co.uk
Did you have a great holiday? Is there something on your mind? Whatever it is, let us know! Whether you want to praise, alert us to errors or give us a personal tip – MARCO POLO would be pleased to hear from you.
We do everything we can to provide the very latest information for your trip. Nevertheless, despite all of our authors' thorough research, errors can creep in. MARCO POLO does not accept any liability for this. Please contact us by e-mail or post.

MARCO POLO Travel Publishing Ltd
Pinewood, Chineham Business Park
Crockford Lane, Chineham
Basingstoke, Hampshire RG24 8AL
United Kingdom

CREDITS
Cover photograph: Westminster Bridge with Big Ben (Look/age fotostock); photos: Corbis/Reuters: S. Newman (18 bottom); R. Freyer (96); Getty Images: D. M. Benett (22), DaniloAndjus (3), O. Donmaz (19 bottom), T. C. French (64), Maremagnum (82/83); Getty Images/Redferns: G. Stewart (115); Getty Images/WireImage: J. Ok pako (87); GuerrillaGardening.org: Richard Reynolds (18 top); huber-images: M. Carassale (14/15), R. Cattini (132/133), J. Foulkes (49, 56), Kremer (54/55), H. P. Merten (4 bottom, 26/27, 118/119), M. Rellini (38, 120 top), R. Taylor (Klappe links, 34, 43, 59, 120 bottom); Laif: G. Azumendi (45), T. Kierok (116), S. Multhaupt (106), M. Sasse (9, 62/63, 90, 121), D. Schwelle (2, 68); Laif/Loop Images: B. Allsopp (37), Q. Bargate (12/13), R. Leaver (112), S. Montgomery (11), E. Nathan (67); Laif/Polaris: D. Leal-Olivas (116/117), S. Lock (60/61), D. Tacon (92/93); Laif/robertharding: M. Lange (40); Look/age fotostock (1); mauritius images: S. Vidler (78, 118, 119), J. Warburton-lee/J. Sweeney (6); mauritius images/age (5, 17, 30); mauritius images/Alamy: (7, 8, 10, 19 top, 51, 70 right, 74, 81, 94), S. Turner (99); mauritius images/Axiom Photographic: C. Bowman (flap rechts); mauritius images/Cultura: W. Perugini (100/101); mauritius images/foodcollection (70 l.); mauritius images/imagebroker/XYZ Pictures (32); mauritius images/Loop Images: T. Anggamulia (24); mauritius images/United Archives (89); mauritius images/View Pictures: (77, 84), G. Smith (72/73); mauritius images/Westend61: A. Pacek (117); picture-alliance/dpa (4 top, 20/21); vario images/TipsImages (71); Visum: M. Theiner (18 centre)

4th Edition 2019 – fully revised and updated
Worldwide Distribution: Marco Polo Travel Publishing Ltd, Pinewood, Chineham Business Park, Crockford Lane, Basingstoke, Hampshire RG24 8AL, United Kingdom. Email: sales@marcopolouk.com
© MAIRDUMONT GmbH & Co. KG, Ostfildern
Chief editor: Marion Zorn; author: Kathleen Becker, co-author: Birgit Weber; editor: Jochen Schürmann; programme supervision: Stephan Dürr, Lucas Forst Gill, Susanne Heimburger, Nikolai Michaelis, Martin Silbermann Kristin Wittemann; picture editor: Gabriele Forst Anja Schlatterer; What's Hot: wunder media, Munich; cartography street atlas: © MAIRDUMONT, Ostfildern; cartography pull-out map: © MAIRDUMONT, Ostfildern; front cover, pull-out map cover, page 1: Karl Anders – Büro für Visual Stories, Hamburg; design: milchhof:atelier, Berlin; design p. 2/3, Discovery Tours: Susan Chaaban Dipl.-Des. (FH)
No part of this book may be reproduced, stored in a retrieval system or transmitted in any form or by any means (electronic, mechanical, photocopying, recording or otherwise) without prior written permission from the publisher.
Translated from German by Susan Jones, Ronit Jariv and Tom Ashforth
Prepress: Nazire Ergün, Cologne
Printed in China

MIX
Paper from responsible sources
FSC® C124385
www.fsc.org

DOS & DON'TS ✌

Don't be caught out; we tell you how

DRIVING

It is not a good idea to take the car to town: a confusing road network, heavy traffic, horrendous park house fees (up to £40 per day). The city is full of speed traps – and many London drivers have short fuses. Last but not least: the city-centre congestion charge, introduced in 2003.

BLOCK THE ESCALATORS

Londoners are often in a hurry. Remember to leave a gap on the underground escalators for those in a rush to catch their next train: The rule is "stand on the right, walk on the left".

PLEASE

Never forget to add a "please" to every order you place in a shop or a restaurant. It is not only polite, but failing to do so is an affront to English ears.

STICKING TO THE TOURIST TRAIL

Visitors just ticking off Madame Tussauds waxworks, the Tower of London, Big Ben, the thronged hubs of Leicester Square and Piccadilly Circus will remain amongst themselves, i. e. in the company of other tourists. You will see more of the real London if you get off the beaten track, take an unfamiliar side street, try an exotic street snack or enter a quirky old-fashioned shop.

JUMP INTO ANY LD MINICAB

When it's a rainy evening and no black cab in sight, the temptation to board any minicab touting for business in the street is very real: *Need a cab?* Be aware of the risks though: unlike the black cabs, whose drivers have to have completed the *Knowledge*, more or less anyone can register a minicab. Drivers often speak little English and may not know the area well. There have also been cases of passengers being attacked.

QUEUE-JUMPING

While the cliché that two Brits immediately form an orderly queue upon meeting no longer really holds true, Londoners do care about a fair order of service, so you're best checking where the end of the queue is.

HAVE A QUICK ONE ON THE TUBE

As part of the effort to fight antisocial behaviour in public, consuming alcohol on buses, on the underground and at stations has been banned since 2008. And compliance with the ban, which covers tourists as well as residents, is strictly controlled.